Glidermen of Neptune

The American D-Day Glider Attack

Charles J. Masters

Southern Illinois University Press
Carbondale and Edwardsville

Copyright © 1995 by the Board of Trustees,
Southern Illinois University
98 97 96 95   4 3 2 1
All rights reserved
Printed in the United States of America
Designed by Edward D. King
Production supervised by Natalia Nadraga

Library of Congress Cataloging-in-Publication Data

Masters, Charles J., date.
    Glidermen of Neptune : the American D-Day
glider attack / Charles J. Masters.
        p.   cm.
    Includes bibliographical references and index.

    1. World War, 1939–1945—Aerial operations.
American. 2. Gliders (Aeronautics). 3. World War,
1939–1945—Campaigns—France—Normandy. 4.
Normandy (France)—History, Military. I. Title.
D790.M345   1995
940.54'4973—dc20   95-11452
                                          CIP
ISBN 0-8093-2007-X
ISBN 0-8093-2008-8 pbk.

Frontispiece: Interior view of a Horsa glider.
(Silent Wings Museum)

The paper used in this publication meets the minimum
requirements of American National Standard for Information Sciences—Permanence of Paper for Printed
Library Materials. ANSI Z39.48-1984. ⊚

Cover illustration: glider attack on D-Day (National Archives);
inset, glidermen await takeoff for Normandy (Silent Wings
Museum).

For my son, Ben; and in memory
of my grandfather Ben, the best
and wisest man I ever knew

Where is the Prince who can afford so to cover his country with troops for its defense, as that 10,000 men, descending from the clouds, might not, in many places, do an infinite deal of mischief before a force could be brought together to repel them?

—Benjamin Franklin, 1784

Contents

Plates

Plates

Preface

THIS BOOK tells the story of the American D-Day glider assault and the circumstances that led up to that moment in history. It is the story of the brave soldiers who made the dangerous cross-Channel attack into Normandy aboard combat gliders—the first stealth weapons of modern warfare. Like other soldiers who fought World War II, these "glidermen" were engaged, ultimately, in a decisive struggle between freedom and oppression. Nothing less than the future of all humankind was at stake. Their war was also the first highly mechanized and armored conflict on a global scale, and thus it remains a fascinating subject to students of history. Besides the enormous effect World War II has had on the geopolitical landscape of the modern world, it also brought about developments in military technology that eclipsed anything devised in previous wars.

By the end of the war, heavily armed fighter planes had been built that could fly at speeds in excess of 400 mph and they engaged in aerial dogfights using tactics and firepower that far surpassed those of the frail biplanes of World War I. Tanks carried more armor and more lethal weaponry than their predecessors had possessed less than a decade before. The static trench warfare of World War I had given way to lightning warfare, or blitzkrieg, as it was so brilliantly executed by the German war machine. And the frontline combat soldier was confronted with an array of weapons never before seen on the battlefield.

In contrast to most of these other developments in warfare, there was no precedent for the combat glider. Prior to World War II no one had ever flown a glider into action. Combat gliders were a singular feature of that war and almost certainly will never be used again. The history of their use spans only about five years, a brief but critical time when no other means existed for the airborne delivery of combat-ready soldiers and equipment to the battlefield. Gliders have since been replaced by helicopters that can carry soldiers and weaponry directly to their objective—a combat tactic that was developed and refined in Vietnam.

The glider assault on Normandy was a daring, all-or-nothing gambit in which the largest gliderborne force ever assembled sought to breach the Atlantic Wall of Hitler's Fortress Europe and seize a foothold in his captive empire. It was to be a perilous attack aboard fragile, wooden or cloth-covered, armorless, and engineless aircraft that were vulnerable to being battered by the wind. They would soar so low over enemy strongholds as to become easy targets for antiaircraft and even small-arms fire. And they would complete their one-way flight by crashing into heavily defended enemy territory.

These combat soldiers known as glidermen were men who went to war aboard gliders that were called "flying coffins" and "tow targets." I first learned about them from my father. He was a gliderman in the Headquarters Company, 2nd Battalion, 325th Glider Infantry Regiment, 82nd Airborne Division. Dad fought with the other glidermen of the 82nd Airborne in North Africa, Sicily, Italy, and in the Normandy invasion. He went to the Normandy battlefield in a CG-4A Waco glider that took off from a field in Upottery in Devonshire, England, 7 June 1944. On 19 June he led a patrol as the point of his battalion in the assault on Pont-l'Abbé, France. Dad was wounded in battle that day, spent three weeks in the hospital, and then returned to his battalion. On 17 August 1944 he received his Glider Badge—the same one that appears in the book. In September he was wounded a second time and this time spent eleven months in the hospital.

I will always be grateful to my father for the many things he taught me. Were it not for him, this book would never have been written. I wish he were alive to read it.

In writing this book, I sought out many glidermen, glider pilots, and troop carrier men who had participated in the actions described in these pages. In the course of my research I was able to locate and speak to 106 of them. Each man, without exception, took the time to answer my many questions or to put me in touch with someone who had the answers, both here and in England. I wish to express my sincere appreciation to all of them.

I particularly want to take the opportunity to thank the glidermen of the 325 Glider Infantry Association, an active and vibrant organization. The men to whom I spoke answered my questions patiently, furnished facts and details, and filled in many gaps in my account. My thanks also go to those members who were in attendance at the 325 reunion in Springfield, Illinois, and who were so gracious and kind as to grant me interviews and furnish me with additional documentation.

Among the published accounts of combat gliders that I used in my research, I should mention two that proved to be particularly useful for pinning down some of the technical details. These were James Mrazek's *The Glider War* and Gerard Devlin's *Silent Wings*. Also I wish to express my gratitude to the National Air and Space Museum, Smithsonian Institution; the National Archives; the St. Louis Mercantile Library; the 82nd Airborne Division War Memorial Museum at Fort Bragg, North Carolina; the Donald F. Pratt Memorial Museum-101st Airborne Division at Fort Campbell, Kentucky; and the Imperial War Museum, London.

Finally, my eternal thanks goes to the Silent Wings Museum, its officers and members, and its curator, James McCord. Jim tirelessly sifted through hundreds of photographs, helped me select from among them and get processed many of those that now appear in this book, and greatly assisted in putting me in contact with glidermen and glider pilots. I urge anyone who is interested in this history to visit the museum, located in Terrell, Texas. It is dedicated to the memory of all World War II airborne personnel and has on display one of only two remaining, completely restored CG-4A gliders in the world.

—Charles J. Masters
Chicago, Illinois

Map 1
Operation Overlord

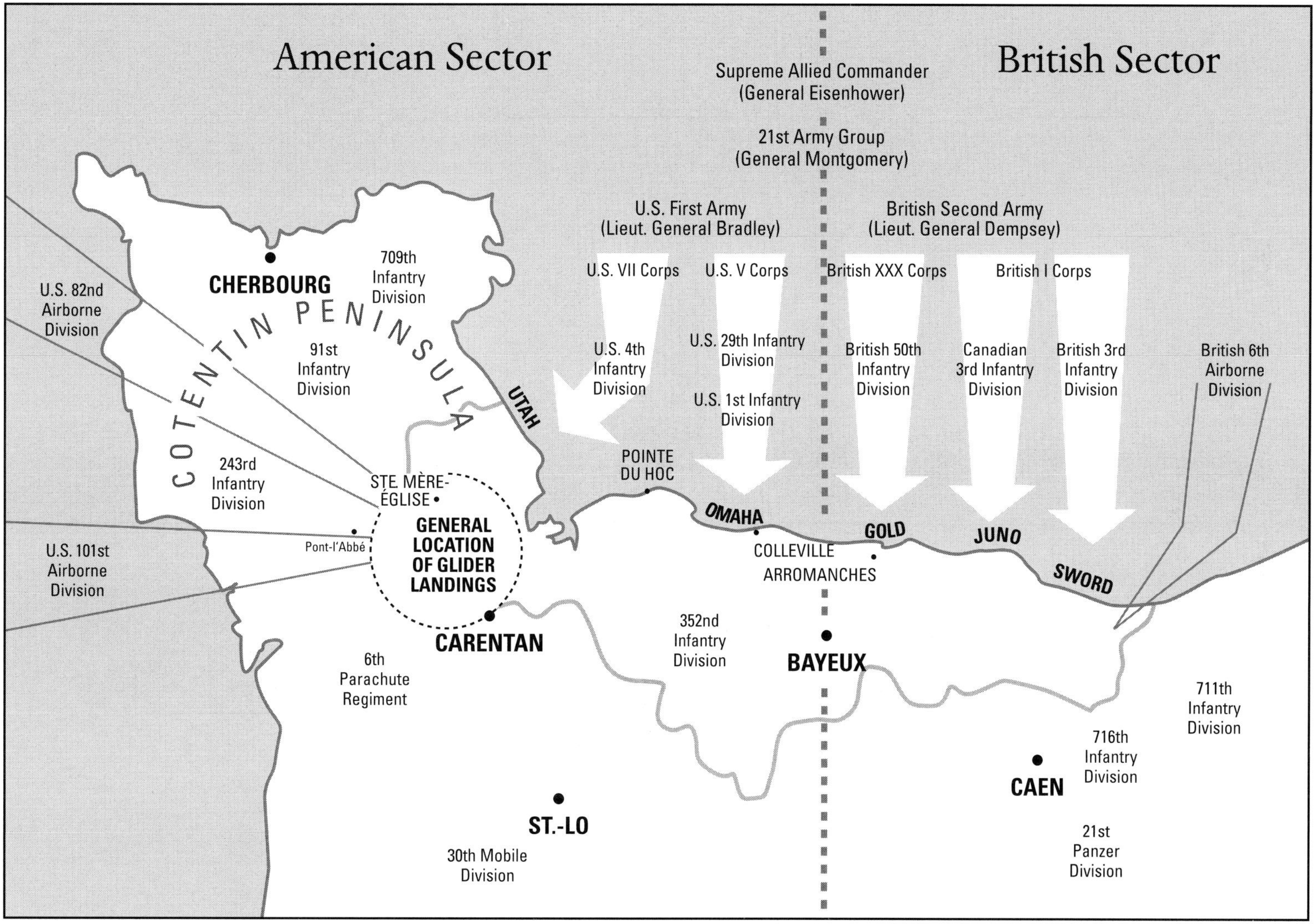

American Sector

British Sector

Supreme Allied Commander
(General Eisenhower)

21st Army Group
(General Montgomery)

British Second Army
(Lieut. General Dempsey)

U.S. First Army
(Lieut. General Bradley)

U.S. VII Corps

U.S. V Corps

British XXX Corps

British I Corps

British 6th
Airborne
Division

711th
Infantry
Division

716th
Infantry
Division

21st Panzer
Division

CAEN

SWORD

British 3rd
Infantry
Division

JUNO

Canadian
3rd Infantry
Division

GOLD

British 50th
Infantry
Division

BAYEUX

ARROMANCHES

COLLEVILLE

OMAHA

U.S. 29th Infantry
Division

U.S. 1st Infantry
Division

352nd
Infantry
Division

POINTE
DU HOC

U.S. 4th
Infantry
Division

UTAH

ST.-LO

30th Mobile
Division

CHERBOURG

709th
Infantry
Division

91st
Infantry
Division

COTENTIN PENINSULA

STE MÈRE-
ÉGLISE

GENERAL
LOCATION
OF GLIDER
LANDINGS

CARENTAN

6th
Parachute
Regiment

243rd
Infantry
Division

Pont-l'Abbé

U.S. 82nd
Airborne
Division

U.S. 101st
Airborne
Division

Map 2
The American Glider Route in the Normandy Invasion

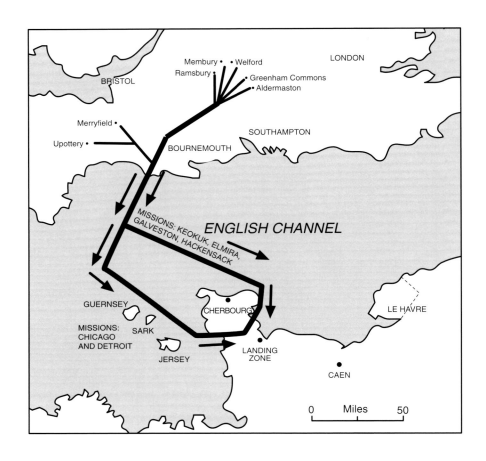

Glidermen of Neptune

American glidermen charge out of a CG-4A glider. (Silent Wings Museum)

A Secret Weapon Enters the War

IN THE HISTORY of the world there has never been a more comprehensive military offensive than the Allied invasion of Normandy, France. For over fifty years military planners and historians alike have marveled not only at the sheer magnitude of the plan but also at the spectacular degree of success achieved in its execution. Even when measured by today's standards and technology, the invasion of Normandy was nothing short of remarkable. No comparable operation had ever been attempted; therefore, the crafting of an invasion plan against such a tenacious and formidable enemy was a task of unprecedented nature. Indeed, the number of details that had to be addressed was so massive and the technical problems so monumental that the invasion plan required thousands of men over a year to complete.

"Operation Overlord" was the code name given the blueprint for the invasion of Hitler's Fortress Europe. And although the evolution of the plan's numerous phases took over a year, almost from its inception the concept anticipated an airborne element with the seaborne campaign. The value of an airborne role was so well appreciated that its employment was almost assured even before an appropriate location for the invasion had been identified. The Allied commanders were acutely aware of the benefits that a successful gliderborne force could add to an attempted seaborne penetration. The D-Day glider attacks would be part of the assault phase that was given the code name "Operation Neptune." Operation Neptune would therefore launch Operation Overlord.

Nevertheless, prior to Operation Neptune the use of gliders in combat was so limited that only a few years earlier many considered them to be a new secret weapon. Combat gliders had such a short military history that their strengths and shortcomings were still being learned while Overlord was being planned. This lack of a full comprehension of the attributes and drawbacks of the glider's use contributed to some heated debates between various commanders during the planning stages.

In truth, combat gliders are not some kind of military aberration but are instead a singular feature of World War II. History reveals that the entire life of combat gliders ranged no more than approximately a dozen years. Yet combat gliders filled a void that military planners faced when contemplating the movement of combat soldiers and matériel. One must bear in mind that no helicopters were used during World War II. Until the use of the combat glider there was no method for the airborne delivery to one location of combat-ready teams of troops who would be prepared to immediately engage the enemy as a unified group. This task could not be accomplished by parachute drop. Quite often soldiers dropped by parachute found that they had landed not only far from their intended drop zone but also substantial distances from one another. Stealth, swiftness, and surprise were required to equalize the balance between the lightly armed paratroopers and an entrenched

Glidermen of the 2nd Battalion, 325th Glider Infantry Regiment, 82nd Airborne Division, loading a 75 mm pack howitzer into a CG-4A glider at Upottery Field, England, 4 June 1944. (Silent Wings Museum)

enemy ground force. The time that was lost attempting to locate one another and organize into an effective combat force could substantially effect the outcome of a mission.

Additionally, there was still no reliable way to accomplish airborne delivery of the larger essential equipment required by paratroopers when they hit the ground. Equipment dropped by parachute was significantly limited in size and weight and was subject to landing far from the drop zone of the paratrooper. If the parachute-dropped equipment could not be located and secured immediately, its intended utility in a mission was rendered useless. The success or failure in achieving a particular objective could depend upon the timely recovery of all or some of the equipment that a commander deemed to be vital. Furthermore, even though parachute-dropped equipment might be located by paratroopers, the time required to retrieve it could jeopardize the success of a mission.

A new dimension in delivery capability was brought to the battlefield by the combat glider, which had the capacity to carry light artillery pieces, jeeps, radio equipment, medical supplies, and even tanks. Before the advent of combat gliders, paratroopers would have to land, locate one another, and then successfully seize an enemy airfield of sufficient size to enable transport aircraft to bring in the heavier equipment needed to sustain a ground force. The capture of an enemy airfield, however, did not provide any assurances that the paratroopers could hold the airfield until the transport aircraft arrived. The lightly armed paratroopers would have to be prepared to defend the airfield if a counterattack was mounted.

75 mm pack howitzer stowed aboard a CG-4A glider. (Silent Wings Museum)

Ideally, then, the combat glider appeared to be the solution to a problem that had long vexed military commanders. Yet the magnitude of risk to the soldiers, or "glidermen" as they were called, who were being transported into combat was not fully comprehended by some who had the authority to issue orders for their use. Crash and casualty statistics, to the limited extent they were available, were not furnished to the glidermen. Even after the German surrender, American glidermen continued their training in Germany without any mention being made to them of the degree of risk involved in these exercises.

It was in fact the Germans, not the Allies, who first comprehended the potential for utilizing gliderborne forces in selected situations. Not only was Germany early to recognize the advantages of supplementing traditional offensive military tactics with a glider element, it was also the first to implement gliderborne attacks. Initially the results achieved were nothing short of a stunning success. Entirely new strategies had to be devised because there was no comparable, practical experience to suggest the appropriate occasion for using combat gliders. Should gliders be used in conjunction with a parachute drop or should these different techniques be used independently? If used in combination, was there

A Secret Weapon Enters the War

a preferred ratio of gliderborne troops to paratroopers? Could the maximum advantage be obtained by complementing a ground attack with a gliderborne assault or by a combination airborne assault comprised of both gliderborne and paratroop elements? Was there a particular terrain that lent itself most favorably to glider usage? Was there a preferred flying formation for gliders? What were the vulnerabilities of gliders to ground attack from small-arms fire? These and myriad other questions remained unanswered. Speculation on the effectiveness of glider use was abundant but the state of knowledge was, at best, primitive.

Nevertheless, in May 1940 the German military was finally presented with the opportunity to test the viability of gliders in combat during the invasion of Belgium. In order to gain access to Belgium, troops would have to cross the Albert Canal—a most formidable obstacle. Three bridges crossed the canal and each was mined, wired for demolition, and defended by Belgian troops in concrete pillboxes. At the first sign of approaching enemy troops, the bridges were to be blown up. Yet the most imposing obstacle confronting the German troops was the massive Fort Eben Emael.

The most modern fortress in Belgium, Eben Emael was constructed entirely underground, with only concrete cupolas exposed above ground level. The banks of the Albert Canal were almost vertical and were fortified with concrete in strategic places. The fortress was designed to have a commanding view and to be impervious to a ground assault. However, the design of the fort also contained an inherent Achilles heel. Its designers did not foresee the potential threat of an airborne attack; accordingly, it was built with no antiaircraft guns or aerial observation posts. German thinking was audacious and innovative. The imposing fortress blocking the prospective invaders presented what appeared to be a perfect opportunity for a glider attack, and the Germans were quick to seize the initiative. The final plan was as bold as it was brilliant and required precision timing and total surprise. Gliders were to go in first and land on top of their objectives and were to be followed by paratroopers.

The entire German force consisted of just seventy-eight glidermen. The fortress was defended by almost 800 Belgian soldiers. At dawn ten gliders were towed to an elevation of 8,000 feet and released while still over Germany; they then proceeded in total silence and finally landed within yards of their targets. The Belgian defenders were caught entirely off guard, having been denied the usual alarm of airplane-engine noise. Immediately upon landing the glidermen formed a unified combat-ready fighting force. Two of the three bridges were captured undamaged. The invaders, having been able to bring with them enormous amounts of high explosive charges, blew up the casemates, the bombproof chambers in the fortress. What moments before had been an impregnable stronghold in an instant was transformed into a prison of smoke and death for its occupants. The Belgians found themselves trapped in a maze of underground tunnels and passageways, unable to mount a counterattack, let alone a viable defense. Fort Eben Emael surrendered the next day. When the tally was completed, the entire operation had resulted in the death of six German glidermen. Unparalleled in modern military history, the first stealth weapon had arrived. The combat glider had come into its own.

It was Hitler himself who conceived the idea of using gliders against Eben Emael. With the result proving to be such a resounding success, it was axiomatic that he would be a strong proponent of gliders in future operations. Hitler had wanted his new secret weapon to be kept a secret, so only those involved in the planning and execution of the mission knew what was going to transpire. After Hitler was informed of the remarkable victory achieved by his gliders, he imposed even more stringent security measures around details of the glider program and the fort's capture. No German news reports covering the capture of the fort contained any information about the gliders. Even many of Germany's high-ranking officers did not know that gliders had played any role whatsoever in the defeat of the Belgian fortress.

The outcome of the Eben Emael attack confirmed the fact that the defensive strategies of World War I were antiquated and were destined to play a reduced role against the modern stratagems of World War II. The rapidity with which the Germans had decimated the Belgian defenses shocked and confounded Allied generals. With the secret of the gliders so carefully guarded, Allied speculation grew rampant. Some thought poison gas must have been used, while others considered sabotage of the fort a possibility. In any case, the Allies' ignorance of the use of the gliders only enhanced their value to Hitler's war machine and relegated Allied intelligence to mere conjecture.

Although Hitler craved more quick and relatively cheap victories, it would be another year before a further opportunity presented itself to the German glidermen. The time came in May 1941. The target was Crete, the largest of the Greek Islands, which lies approximately sixty-three miles southeast of the mainland. Greece had been overrun by the Germans, and Crete had become the last bastion of safety for the retreating British and Commonwealth troops. In April 1941 Hitler ordered the invasion of Crete, which became the scene of the first large-scale airborne invasion in history. Four hundred paratroop-carrying planes and seventy-two gliders were mustered for the assault.

One of the principle objectives of the attackers was the capture of Maleme airfield. The gliders were to be sent in nearer to the airfield since the glidermen would be ready to engage the enemy faster than the paratroopers would. The paratroopers were supposed to land a mile or two away from the airfield where it was anticipated that enemy resistance would be less intense. Upon landing, the paratroopers would then have the opportunity to organize themselves for an attack.

On 19 May the operation began. First the Luftwaffe relentlessly pounded the Allied defensive positions around the airfield. Soon after the bombing ceased, the glidermen were sent in. This time, however, the saga played out with a different result. The gliders encountered difficulties even before they landed and never achieved the requisite element of surprise. The defenders opened fire with everything in their arsenal on the unarmed invading craft. The gliders sustained a vicious bombardment of rifle and machine-gun fire. Some gliders hit trees and ripped apart while others smashed into the ground. A number of the gliders that succeeded in setting down more or less intact were so riddled with bullets that all the glidermen inside were dead upon landing. Other glidermen were killed by the defenders as they tried to escape their gliders. To make matters worse, German intelligence reports had misjudged the suitability of certain glider landing zones—actually, terraced hills that gliders smashed straight into, spreading bodies, guns, and ammunition boxes all over. At Maleme airfield the gliders landed with a reasonable degree of accuracy, albeit many crashed.

The glidermen who did survive the torrent of gunfire and the chaotic landings proceeded to fight the defenders tenaciously. Nevertheless, the losses to the gliderborne force in wounded and dead and in aircraft and equipment were brutal. Compounding these losses, the paratroopers also sustained heavy casualties. Altogether the German attacking force amounted to 22,000 men, of whom approximately 4,000 were killed and 2,000 were wounded. All the gliders and 170 of the air transports were destroyed.

British and Commonwealth losses were even worse. The battle raged until the commander of their troops, Maj. Gen. B. C. Freyberg, finally made the decision to evacuate Crete. For four nights the Royal Navy rescued as many of the 42,500 defenders as possible, suffering heavy losses in the process. Three cruisers and six destroyers were sunk and thirteen other ships were severely damaged, including the fleet's only aircraft carrier, and more than 2,000 seamen were killed. About 16,500 men were evacuated, including approximately 2,000 Greeks. Four thousand British troops were killed, 2,500 were wounded, and 12,000 were left behind and captured. Moreover, 10,000 Greek and Cretan irregulars and Cypriot troops were also captured by the Germans and all the British equipment on Crete fell into German hands.

The Germans had satisfied their objective of taking Crete; notwithstanding their losses, it was a monumental victory for them. The Crete exploit evinced, as no other campaign had ever done, the effectiveness of a properly used airborne element. Still, their huge losses, coupled with Hitler's belief that gliders were too dangerous to use without the advantage of surprise, brought to an end the German glider effort, with the exception of some minor operations undertaken later in the war. Combat gliders had proven too hazardous and costly for them.

Although the German military based this conclusion upon the Crete experience, that same experience also signaled the very beginning of the Allied glider effort. It was now the

The Airspeed AS 51 Horsa glider. Made by the British, it was constructed almost entirely of plywood. This Horsa was used by U.S. glidermen and bears American markings. (U.S. Air Force Photo Collection [USAF Neg. No. A 80300 AC], courtesy of National Air and Space Museum, Smithsonian Institution)

Allies who perceived a state of affairs to be ripe for an airborne assault consisting of paratroop and gliderborne forces. Their objective was the invasion of Sicily, code-named "Operation Husky." In sheer numbers Husky would be the greatest amphibious assault of the war to that time, involving nearly half a million men. The decision to invade Sicily was made in January 1943. Plans called for the British 8th Army to seize five points on the southeastern tip of Sicily and for the U.S. 7th Army to take three beaches to the west of the British forces. It was determined that an airborne assault would be an essential ingredient, and the assignment was given to the British 1st Airborne Division and the American 82nd Airborne Division.

The American 82nd Airborne consisted of the 504th and 505th Parachute Infantry Regiments and the 325th Glider Infantry Regiment. Transport was to be accomplished by the 12th Troop Carrier Command consisting of 331 C-47s. The British 1st Airborne was composed of the 1st and 2nd Parachute Brigades and one Air Landing Brigade. However, the British had virtually no transport aircraft and few gliders. In fact, only nineteen British gliders, known as Horsas, had been successfully towed to the North African staging area for Operation Husky.

The British-built Airspeed AS 51 Horsa glider was made almost entirely of plywood and was significantly larger than its American counterpart. Measuring 68 feet long, almost 20 feet high, and with a wingspan of 88 feet, a Horsa could carry 28 fully equipped, combat-ready glidermen or up to 7,000 pounds of matériel, such as a jeep and a 75 mm pack howitzer, or two jeeps, or a jeep and a trailer. Fully loaded a Horsa weighed more than seven tons and could carry a weight almost equal to its own in glidermen or equipment.

Britain commenced production of the Horsas in June 1942 and built more than 5,000 by the end of the war. The decision to construct the Horsas out of plywood was primarily based upon the type of factories in Britain that had available production capacity during

Interior view of a Horsa glider. (Silent Wings Museum)

the war. However, it was also imperative that the selected factories not be needed in the construction of other military aircraft. Accordingly, furniture factories were designated as production sites since they were not involved in work considered vital to the national war effort.

Cut into the fuselage of the Horsa were two doors that ran up into the roof on slides. These doors could be opened while the glider was still in flight and were originally designed to permit paratroop assaults or to enable the glidermen to use machine guns to defend themselves against fighter attacks—an idea that proved to be utterly impractical and was never used. In addition to the two sliding doors, there was a freight-loading door on the port side of the glider, just to the rear of the cockpit. For loading and unloading, the door hinged downwards and the equipment was pushed in and out on two ramps. By a stroke of luck, it turned out that an American-made jeep could just squeeze past the door posts and be pushed in.

During combat landings, however, it took too much precious time to unload a jeep through the cargo door. Accordingly, two modifications were made to the Horsa to effectuate quick unloading. The first and easiest way was to blow the tail off. Each tail section was fitted with explosive ring charges that the glidermen could trigger. After the explosion the glidermen could push aside the tail, exposing the wide-open fuselage. The second, less-favored method involved removing the tail section by unscrewing six large bolts that held it in place. In enemy territory the glidermen almost always detonated the implanted cord charges rather than fiddled with the bolts.

The tail of this Horsa glider, which landed safely on D-Day, was blown off by triggering a cordtex explosive ring charge to permit rapid unloading of equipment. The ramp used to unload it was carried on board. (U.S. Air Force Photo Collection [USAF Neg. No. 116014 AC], courtesy of National Air and Space Museum, Smithsonian Institution)

The plywood construction of the Horsas only served to enhance their reputation as "flying coffins" among the glidermen, who tended to favor the American-made CG-4A Waco as the glider of choice. If they were to be towed to the battlefield in a flying coffin, they thought that at least it should be done in a coffin chosen by the men riding inside. In comparison to the Horsa, the Waco was smaller and easier to fly and maintain. Forty-eight feet long and with a wingspan of 83.6 feet, the Waco was designed to carry ten fully equipped, combat-ready glidermen, or a 75 mm howitzer with its crew of glidermen, or a jeep with its crew.

Glidermen of Neptune

The American-made CG-4A Waco glider. (U.S. Air Force Photo Collection [USAF Neg. No. 75950 AC], courtesy of National Air and Space Museum, Smithsonian Institution)

Interior view of a CG-4A glider. Note the two control wheels and minimal instrumentation. (Author's Collection)

The Waco was a good cargo carrier but because of its smaller size had the inherent limitation that it could not carry both a howitzer and the jeep needed to make it mobile. Therefore, two gliders were required to deliver a howitzer, a towing jeep, and the glidermen who operated them. The square fuselage of the Waco was made of tubular steel covered with nothing more than canvas. The floor was a plywood honeycomb design, and the wings and tail were also constructed of wood and fabric. A total of 13,900 CG-4As and CG-4s, a design variation, were built. Of these, approximately 8,500 were delivered to various theaters of war, the vast majority being destined for Europe.

The aircraft designated to tow the Wacos into combat was the C-47, the military version of the DC-3 that had flown as a civil airliner since 1935. The C-47 had twin engines (1,200 hp Pratt and Whitney Twin Wasps) that could attain a maximum speed of 230 mph

A Secret Weapon Enters the War

The twin-engine C-47 used to tow gliders. (Silent Wings Museum)

and a cruising speed of 167 mph. It was a well designed and durable aircraft that had a range of 1,300 miles and a crew of three. From 1939 through 1945, the C-47 provided the backbone of both the American and British military air transport services and was used in every theater of the war. With a load capacity of 9,028 pounds, it was ideal for towing both Wacos and Horsas into combat. The C-47, however, was completely unarmed. The British aircraft used to tow their Horsas were Albemarles and Halifaxes. However, due to the shortage of these aircraft the C-47s often had to do the towing for the Horsas. When used by the British, the C-47 was called the "Dakota."

Operation Husky called for a two-prong assault, with the British attacking the southeastern segment of Sicily and the Americans attacking the southwestern segment. Both British and American landings were planned to take place at dusk. This would permit a full night for the troops and equipment to get ashore and assemble and, it was hoped, would avert enemy air attacks. The combined Allied force would then attack northward up the island. The ultimate objective was to invade Italy itself by crossing the Strait of Messina from the northeastern tip of the island.

The airborne forces were intended to set down inland from the beaches in order to block the enemy from sending reinforcements against the Allied troops invading the beaches. The American landings on the southwest were to be protected by the 505th Parachute Infantry Regiment, reinforced by the 504th Regiment if needed. The British assignment at the southeast corner of the island required that the road north from the beachhead area to Syracuse be taken. The only way to accomplish this objective was to take control of the Ponte Grande Bridge, about a mile and a half southwest of Syracuse. Thereafter, the Syracuse harbor, which was only half a mile from the bridge, was to be captured and a coastal battery that could strike the invasion beaches was to be eliminated.

Because of the shortage of Horsas, Wacos were made available to the British. On the night of 9 July, the British marshaled 144 aircraft consisting of 109 Dakotas, 28 Albermarles, and 7 Halifaxes to tow 136 Wacos and 8 Horsas against Syracuse. A force of 1,200 glidermen from the British Air Landing Brigade ascended in their gliders. A strong, 40 mph wind was blowing from the southeast, raising clouds of dust from the airfields, hammering the fragile gliders, and banging around the glidermen inside. The gliders were to be released

One of the many Allied gliders that crash-landed in the sea during the invasion of Sicily, 10 July 1943. (U.S. Air Force Photo Collection [USAF Neg. No. 26827 AC], courtesy of National Air and Space Museum, Smithsonian Institution)

over the water and make their way quietly over the beaches to their designated landing zones. A high risk adventure, the mission got into trouble almost immediately.

Poor visibility due to the darkness, a difficult, bending flight path, and battering winds contributed to the problems encountered by the tow pilots. Some of the gliders and their towing aircraft fell out of formation. A few gliders never got very far and released early in an attempt to return to their airfields. In one case the turbulence was so severe that a jeep came loose and began to slam and smash into the interior of the glider, tearing it to shreds from the inside. Many gliders were released too soon and never made it to land. Of the 144 gliders that started out, at least sixty-nine crashed into the sea. Two hundred fifty-two men were known to have drowned. At least ten more gliders that were missing and unaccounted for also probably crashed into the sea, with the loss of all their glidermen. Some glider pilots never saw the shore or failed to recognize any inland landmarks and missed their landing zones completely. Many that did make it over land crashed into trees, stone walls, or the ground itself. Of the fifty-two gliders that actually made it to Sicily, it is estimated that only about a dozen landed near their prescribed targets.

A glider mission over enemy territory under even the most favorable conditions would have been problematic, but the military planners had completely underestimated the perils of a release of gliders over water in the dark. Although Husky was a military success, the hazards inherent in a glider attack were becoming ever more pronounced. While the American command was starting to grasp the value of combat gliders, the American glidermen who would take their turn on D-Day in Normandy and thereafter in Holland had little appreciation for the magnitude of danger they faced. They certainly did not know that from its inception the program for the development of the Waco was disorganized and possibly negligent and that some of their gliders were defective from the moment they came off American assembly lines.

The terrible losses suffered by the German gliders at Crete had been sufficient to convince Hitler—although apparently not the Allied commanders—that the jeopardies of glider warfare were intolerable. The Allied command also knew about the devastation of the British gliderborne force at Sicily, but that information was not shared with the American glidermen preparing for their assault on Normandy. Moreover, neither the German glidermen attacking Crete nor the British glidermen attacking Sicily had been confronted with the combination of harsh natural defenses and a grisly network of antiglider devices that the American glidermen would face on D-Day.

A Secret Weapon Enters the War

2

A C-47 takes off with two CG-4A gliders in tow. As can be seen, the gliders gain altitude faster than the tow plane. (Imperial War Museum, London)

The American Combat-Glider Program Takes Off

WHEN THE UNITED STATES entered World War I against Germany on 6 April 1917, the 82nd Division had not even been formed. It commenced its existence as a conventional infantry division at Camp Gordon, Georgia on 25 August 1917. By the time World War I ended, less than two years later, the 82nd Division had participated in three major campaigns, had seen more continuous days of combat than any other U.S. division, and had suffered almost seventy-five percent casualties. The first contingent of the 82nd sailed for Europe on 20 April 1918. Passing through England en route to France, the 82nd's 325th Infantry Regiment was reviewed by His Majesty the King. The 82nd relieved the 2nd Division on 15 August and was then joined by the 157th Artillery Brigade, which gave the division its own artillery support rather than its having to rely on the heavy guns of the French.

The division was chosen to participate in the first major U.S. offensive of the war at St.-Mihiel, where the objective was the village of Norroy. Meeting no heavy resistance, the Americans seized the town; however, 950 casualties were sustained during the campaign which lasted until 21 September 1918. In this battle Lt. Col. Emory Pike earned a Medal of Honor, awarded to him posthumously. On 24 September the division moved to the Clermont region west of Verdun, which was the local site of the Meuse-Argonne Offensive, one of the bloodiest engagements in military history. During its participation in this offensive alone, the 82nd Division suffered more than 7,400 casualties. It also produced the most celebrated American soldier of the war, Cpl. Alvin C. York.

The division earned the nickname "All Americans" from the fact that it was composed of men from every state in the Union. The Armistice went into effect on 11 November 1918 and the All Americans were deactivated as a division on 27 May 1919. In addition to the division's two Medals of Honor recognizing Pike and York, three other All Americans earned the Distinguished Service Medal and seventy-five were awarded the Distinguished Service Cross.

The outbreak of World War II triggered the reactivation of the 82nd on 25 March 1942, at Camp Claiborne, Louisiana, under the command of Brig. Gen. (later, Maj. Gen.) Omar Bradley. He was an exceptional strategist and leader who inspired the confidence not only of his superiors but also of his men and he came to be known as the "GI's general." A protege and classmate of Eisenhower at West Point, Bradley was chosen by Eisenhower to command the American landings on Normandy on D-Day. Bradley's second in command was Brig. Gen. Matthew B. Ridgway, who on 26 June 1942 became division commander. A daring and dynamic leader, Ridgway was involved in organizing the airborne landing portion of the assault on Sicily in 1943. Still later, on D-Day, he would lead his 82nd in the assault on the Cotentin Peninsula. When Ridgeway was given command of the 82nd, Bradley was given the assignment of trying to resuscitate a weak National Guard division.

At one point the War Department contemplated training the All Americans as a motorized division. Instead, on 10 August 1942 Ridgeway broke the news to his men that the 82nd Infantry Division was to be reorganized into the first airborne division in American history and was to be redesignated the 82nd Airborne. Concurrently, half the division's men were to be drawn off to form a second airborne division and designated the 101st Airborne. Thus commenced the life of two of the most famous divisions of any army in World War II. Among the initial units assigned to the 82nd Airborne Division were the 325th and the 326th Glider Infantry Regiments, the 504th Parachute Infantry Regiment, the 319th and the 320th Glider Field Artillery Battalions, the 376th Parachute Field Artillery Battalion, the 80th Airborne Antiaircraft Battalion, and the 307th Airborne Engineer Battalion.

Originally, the two new divisions were relatively small, consisting of approximately 8,500 men as opposed to 14,000 men in a standard infantry division of the time. Under this plan of organization, each division was supposed to have two glider infantry regiments and one parachute infantry regiment. This was changed, however, to provide each division with one glider infantry and two parachute infantry regiments, due in part to the shortage of gliders. Consequently, in February 1943 the 505th Parachute Infantry replaced the 326th Glider Infantry Regiment. While typical infantry regiments were composed of 3,000 men, the regiments of these new divisions had less than 2,000. Artillery for each new division consisted of thirty-six 75 mm pack howitzers and an allotment of 647 vehicles, significantly less than the standard division allocation. As the war progressed the divisional strength was increased to 13,000 men, which brought them closer in size to other, standard infantry divisions.

Although the U.S. command was not privy to the details of the capture of Fort Eben Emael in Belgium, there was speculation that glidermen had played a role in the mission. U.S. military intelligence accumulated various fragments of data suggesting that Germany had constructed gliders and had some experience training with them. Although the data were sketchy at best, they pointed to the conclusion that Germany most likely had an operational gliderborne force of some size. The measure of the force in numbers of gliders, glider pilots, and trained glidermen, as well as what actually constituted the training, was unknown. Nevertheless, the general thinking began to focus on the development of an American glider program.

On 20 February 1941 Gen. Henry H. "Hap" Arnold directed the commencement of the American glider effort. Arnold, who was Chief of the U.S. Army Air Forces, was selected for the task by Army Chief of Staff Gen. George C. Marshall. Arnold, a true aviator to the core, was taught to fly by the Wright brothers in 1911. He commanded the U.S. Army Air Corps in 1938 and was the driving force for the corps' growth from less than 25,000 men and 4,000 aircraft, to over 2,500,000 men and 75,000 aircraft. In June 1941 he became chief of the newly formed United States Army Air Forces, and its commanding general in March 1942. He was a member of the American Joint Chiefs of Staff and Allied Combined Chiefs of Staff during the war. In 1947 the United States Army Air Force was granted independent status and Arnold became its first five-star general.

On 4 March 1941 Arnold gave orders to the Air Corps Experimental Test Center to design a glider with the capacity to transport ten glidermen into combat. From the beginning the program was plagued with false starts, incorrect judgments, and an overabun-

CG-4A glider belonging to the 101st Airborne crashes during exercises on 4 June 1943, after the tow rope breaks and damages the right stabilizer. (National Archives)

dance of disorganization. Time and money were wasted on a myriad of misguided decisions. For example, the effort to build specific types of training gliders, after the fashion of using powered-aircraft trainers, was finally abandoned when it was realized that special training models were not needed. There were also attempts to develop two-man and eight-man gliders since there were no existing criteria for determining the optimum size for a combat glider. Without some historical precedent to build upon, many decisions were made that were little more than educated guesses. Yet due to the pressing demand for gliders and the short time allotted for their delivery, by July 1941 contracts had been executed with no less than sixteen companies for the construction of the CG-4As.

Inasmuch as the military was attempting to prioritize the production of powered air-

The American Combat-Glider Program

The mayor of St. Louis and nine other officials were killed when the wing of this CG-4A glider fell off during a demonstration flight at Lambert Field, St. Louis, Missouri, 1 August 1943. (The St. Louis Mercantile Library)

craft with the available industrial capacity, it was determined that glider contracts should take a subordinate position. Accordingly, the companies retained to manufacture gliders were those not already under contract to produce engine-powered combat planes. The glider program proliferated and in time scores of companies throughout the country were involved in one facet or another. The leading manufacturer, as it turned out, was the Waco Aircraft Company, located in Troy, Ohio. Although a small company, it had been founded in 1921 and had ample experience in producing commercial aircraft. As the primary design contractor, it dealt with other corporations under government contract. In turn, some of these corporations entered into contracts with various subcontractors and material suppliers for various components of the CG-4A. With the program moving fast and growing to include many participants, a diminishing standard in quality was almost an inescapable result.

One contractor was the Robertson Aircraft Corporation of St. Louis, Missouri. A demonstration flight of a CG-4A was scheduled for 1 August 1943, less than eleven months before D-Day. Five thousand people were in attendance at Lambert Field to watch the exhibition. On board the glider were a number of St. Louis executives and dignitaries, including Mayor William Dee Becker. The glider was hitched to the tow plane by a silver-painted tow rope. As the demonstration flight proceeded, a wing abruptly fell off the CG-4A. From an altitude of 2,000 feet, the glider came crashing down, killing all of its passengers. An investigation was immediately undertaken to determine the cause of the disaster. Although sabotage was initially suspected, a careful examination of the wreckage uncovered that a defective part was responsible for the failure. The faulty part was traced to its manufacturer, the Gardner Metal Products Company of St. Louis, one of many subcontracting material suppliers to Robertson Aircraft. Further probing disclosed that the Gardner Company previously had been a coffin manufacturer.

While some CG-4A Wacos were being produced for approximately $15,400 each, other companies were charging the government $25,000 and, in one case, as much as $51,000 apiece for their CG-4As. Although the craft did not appear to be sophisticated, more than 70,000 parts were required to construct each one. One positive attribute of the glider's design was that the entire nose section swung upward as the entry door, which afforded rapid loading and unloading. Unlike the Horsa, the CG-4A was designed to accommodate two pilots side by side. The earliest models had a single control wheel on a column that could be moved in front of either the pilot or the copilot. Subsequent versions provided each pilot with his own control wheel. Instrumentation was sparse, consisting of an altimeter, an airspeed gauge, a rate-of-climb indicator, and a bank-and-turn indicator.

Fully loaded the Waco glider could reach a maximum safe speed of 150 mph, which made it perfectly compatible with the C-47 towing plane. However, there was a conspicuous need for some form of communication between the glider pilot and the tow pilot. One solution that was tried was to stretch a telephone wire between them, which had to be wrapped around the tow rope. This often resulted in the wire either snapping or shorting out. The inability of the two pilots to effectively communicate increased the already considerable hazards they faced, so two-way radios were subsequently employed. However, these too did not always work.

Besides the many, seemingly uncontrollable mortal dangers facing the glidermen on

Loading a jeep into a CG-4A glider at Upottery Field, England, 4 June 1944. (National Archives)

D-Day, including enemy ground fire, a network of menacing antiglider devices, a terrain covered with natural and man-made obstacles, unpredictable air turbulence, and possibly defective glider parts, the glidermen were not issued parachutes. Moreover, there was a shortage of trained glider pilots by the time D-Day arrived and so a gliderman with no actual flight training occupied the copilot's seat, adding to the risk of everyone on board. Some glider pilots in the attack on Normandy were killed before their gliders landed, and whoever happened to be sitting in the copilot's seat had to take on the responsibility of piloting the craft. In the words of Gen. James M. Gavin, "Having to land a glider for the first time in combat is a chastening experience; it gives a man religion."[1]

The availability of qualified glider pilots was a perpetual problem. On 20 December 1941, just thirteen days after the bombing of Pearl Harbor, the required number of glider

1. James M. Gavin, *On to Berlin* (New York: Bantam, 1985), p. 92.

Glidermen practice rapid unloading of a trailer from a CG-4A glider during exercises in England. (Silent Wings Museum)

View of a tow rope and a tow plane from a glider. Telephone cable is wrapped around the tow line for communication between the two craft. (Silent Wings Museum)

pilots was established to be 1,000. The goal of having a 1,000 glider pilots was not arrived at arbitrarily, but it was misguided. The number was chosen in the belief that seventy-five percent of the men and equipment of a standard infantry division could be transported in gliders, while the remainder of the division could be transported in the tow planes themselves.

However, the military soon recognized that the increasing size of the glider-pilot program would interfere with the simultaneously growing power-pilot requirements. With the country at war, 1,000 experienced and trained power pilots could not be afforded. Therefore it was decided that select volunteer enlisted men with prior flying experience would be chosen for the glider-pilot training program. Unfortunately, even this resource did not prove adequate to meet the manpower need. On 1 April 1942 General Arnold ordered that the requirement for glider pilots be increased to 4,200 and then a few weeks later ordered a further increase to 6,000 glider pilots.

The demand for 6,000 glider pilots burdened even the resources of available enlisted men, and the Civil Aeronautics Administration was asked to assist in recruiting pilots from among civilian pilots of both powered and glider aircraft. Nevertheless, neither the efforts of the administration nor the willing enlistment of patriotic civilian pilots could prevent the eventual lowering of the qualifications required of new pilots, to the point that even those who had no prior flying time were accepted for glider-pilot training. In light of the enormous number of trained glider pilots needed and the exigency of the situation, the training facilities at military bases, which were already overencumbered with the demands of training power pilots, were insufficient to the task. As a result glider pilot training was undertaken at civilian schools. While CG-4As were being produced, civilian-owned gliders were purchased together with certain light, powered aircraft that were modified to a non-powered configuration for training purposes.

Inefficiency, poor-quality workmanship, inconsistent construction criteria, and careless planning permeated the glider production program. Meanwhile, glidermen were being inculcated with the notion that going to war in a glider was just another way of being transported into combat—despite the fact that they had to be the consummate combat soldiers, ready to take incalculable risks to reach the battlefield before even engaging the enemy in combat—which they were training and preparing to do aboard their CG-4A Wacos.

3

CG-4A gliders delivered to England for D-Day. Note in the foreground the crated gliders; in the center, the fuselages; and at the top, the fully assembled gliders. (U.S. Air Force Photo Collection [USAF Neg. No. 51194 AC], courtesy of National Air and Space Museum, Smithsonian Institution)

Building Up in Britain for an Airborne Assault

BY APRIL 1944 Britain was engulfed in a fury of activity. Ships were delivering thousands of men and millions of tons of matériel to hundreds of ports around the island. Shipyards were frenetically constructing an array of vessels of all sizes. But shipyards were not the only places where shipbuilding was undertaken. Inland, away from the customary dry docks and port construction facilities, prefabricated craft were assembled in streets, alleys, and warehouses. Scores of thousands of people set about welding, sawing, hammering, riveting, and moving a great host of seagoing vessels.

Assault tanks had to be modified to deal with the multitude of obstacles and traps constructed by the enemy that would confront them during the invasion on the Normandy beaches. The time allotted for training the men to operate these modified assault-vehicles placed an enormous strain on the reservoir of manpower, which was already being stretched to its limits. Men were being instructed in the operation of amphibious vehicles and myriad assault landing-craft and tank-landing craft. At the same time these men trained for the seaborne assault on the beaches, others were training for an airborne assault above and behind the enemy's beaches.

Preparations in Britain by the spring of 1944 had reached such a fever pitch, with so many men, so much matériel, and such an immeasurable amount of official activity, that ordinary civilian activity was almost completely curtailed. While the legions of men and women pursued their assignments, military traffic on both railroads and highways made civilian movement nearly impossible and bottlenecks inevitable. On 10 March 1944 all transportation and communication came under tight control. Except for doctors or others on vital business of national concern, civilians were consigned to traveling on foot or by bicycle. On 6 April all military leave was stopped. Censorship of mail and all other communications was increased to its highest level thus far. By May over 1,500,000 American fighting men were bivouacked in Britain, twice what their number had been at the first of the year.

The Americans brought with them a colossal amount of weaponry, ammunition, equipment, vehicles, food, and other matériel. The island of Britain was absorbing over 750,000 tons of supplies a month. Supplies destined for the Americans had to be routed through certain designated ports, while those supplies assigned to the British had to be funneled through their own allocated ports. The Allies were well aware of the problems that could be encountered if their supply lines were not separately maintained. Each army had its own system of management, organization, and administration, as well as certain types of compatible equipment and supplies. While they attempted to keep lines of supplies and communications separate and distinct—which presented logistical problems of its own—the Allies had to acknowledge one inescapable fact: that two huge armies were poised to attack on the same day, in the same assault, and with a common goal.

Buildup of CG-4A gliders and C-47s. (National Archives)

Concurrent with all the other activity on the island, the American glidermen had been undergoing intensive training, which continued at the same rigorous pace until the middle of May. The glidermen, like other Allied invasion soldiers, became more acutely aware with each passing day that the hour of invasion was coming closer. Still, neither the day nor the time of the assault had been finalized. A phenomenal amount of data remained to be sifted through and analyzed. Decisions had to be made and the potential consequences of these decisions considered, including questions about the phases of the moon and the tides, before launching the largest invasion in history. Although confident that the ultimate day was approaching, the men were starting to get impatient, wanting to get on with the job they had to do so they could return to their own land and to their normal lives as soon as possible.

Although each day occupied the glidermen with the routine of training, sometimes they had the opportunity to relax for an evening in the nearest town. Of course, it was mandatory to obtain a pass, but this was generally not too difficult to arrange. Army trucks furnished the glidermen with the necessary transportation to and from the local villages. Some of the towns were no more than a few miles from the camps, in which case there was the possibility of catching a local bus.

Training and meals still left excess time that needed to be filled, and the modest amount of sports equipment that was available at most of the camps provided a much needed outlet for some of the ever growing, pent-up energy. A good game of tackle football often could be organized on a moment's notice. However, a proliferation of sports injuries resulted in the not completely unexpected order being sent down to end tackle games. Touch games were not so enjoined, although some of them were played with an intensity that was impossible to distinguish from that of tackle. A few baseball gloves, in varying

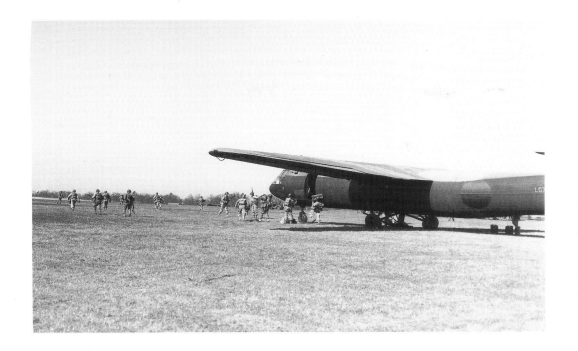

Glidermen unloading a Horsa during training exercises in England. (U.S. Air Force Photo Collection [USAF Neg. No. A 54669 AC], courtesy of National Air and Space Museum, Smithsonian Institution)

conditions, were available, and a baseball, or something similar, and a bat might be found. Playing a game of catch or shagging fly balls helped consume some of the time.

For other men, boxing provided the needed outlet, and boxing teams were organized by company. Boxing matches were scheduled events, each company pitting its best against the others. Boxing gloves always seemed to be available and the contests provided a welcome diversion for the participants, as well as for those who looked for the chance to wager some of their pay. Money, however, was not the exclusive legal tender and a bet could always be made for cigarettes or chocolate bars, whether the betting revolved around a boxing match, a race, or a poker or dice game.

Letters not only provided news from home but also was the only conduit, albeit an irregular one, to family, friends, and loved ones. Envelopes and packages bearing news from home also might contain an extra dollar, a birthday gift, or some requested item, such as a wristwatch, that might not be available at the PX. Letters were read and reread innumerable times. The constant hurry-up-and-wait that is so endemic in the army and the pervasive anticipation of the dangerous exploit about to be undertaken, blended with the training, the living conditions, and the shared uncertainty of when the "Day" would arrive, all served to enhance the camaraderie among the glidermen.

The camps and airfields for the three Allied airborne divisions that would spearhead the Normandy invasion were scattered all over southern England. Nevertheless, the various locations of the U.S. 82nd and 101st Airborne Divisions were relatively concentrated in specific areas, while the camps and airfields of the British 6th Airborne Division were similarly clustered. This configuration sufficed to preserve the autonomy of the two armies and maintained the segregation of their lines of supply.

C-47s fly over Horsa and CG-4A gliders of 101st Airborne during exercises in England. (National Archives)

The tent camp of the 325th Glider Infantry Regiment grew up in an English meadow near the village of Scraptoft, approximately three miles from the city of Leicester, which served as the headquarters of the 82nd Airborne. The main body of the regiment arrived at Scraptoft from Northern Ireland in the early morning hours of 16 February. From then on, through the early spring, the weather was windswept, rain soaked, gray, and bleak. Despite the weather, the nearness to Leicester afforded the men the chance to enjoy the local British hospitality.

During these months housing accommodations consisted of floorless pyramidal tents. Nissen huts were constructed to serve as mess halls and kitchens, and several other comparable structures housed battalion headquarters and the regimental command post. Other improvements were made as time passed, including the building of fences and roads. By the time spring arrived, the 325th camp, which was similar to other airborne camps, had benefited from a significant amount of American "spit and polish."

There was no repose from the training, which was in fact augmented as much as possible within the limitations of the English countryside. In March the 2nd Battalion, 401st Glider Infantry Regiment of the 101st Airborne was attached to the 325th, creating a three-battalion regiment and the need for supplemental coordinated training. There were glider training flights, including an Easter Sunday regimental flight with takeoffs from several southern England airfields, including those near Greenham Commons, Aldermaston, Membury, and Ramsbury. On 8 May a military intelligence interrogation team was attached to the regiment, its purpose being to extract tactical information from the enemy. A practice sealing of the camp was held on 16 May. When passes to town were stopped, it was as clear a sign as the glidermen could expect that the day they had been anticipating was near. In the middle of May the strict regimen of daily training changed to a routine comprised principally of inspections. All personal equipment was checked and rechecked and new equipment was issued for anything that was not in good condition.

On the afternoon of 23 May a heavily guarded two-and-a-half-ton truck under the command of a major pulled up to the situation hut of the 325th camp and stopped. Armed troops immediately surrounded the perimeter of the area. After careful scrutiny, the grounds were deemed to be secure and the order was given to unload boxes containing the maps that the regiment would use for the invasion. Two days later a seaborne contingent of sixty-six men left camp for a marshaling area near Cardiff, Wales. Their assignment was to transport the heavy equipment that could not be flown in by glider.

Every man knew that the day of assault, the hour and the minute they had all trained for so long and so hard, was impending: when they would climb—and in some cases have to be helped up, being so heavily laden with weapons and equipment—into the cramped quarters of a glider; when they would buckle on their safety belts, watch the 300 foot nylon tow rope grow taut as the C-47 thundered down the runway, and feel their glider abruptly lift up, fifteen or thirty seconds before the tow plane left the ground; when they would grab onto anything at hand in the interior of the glider, as it hit air pockets and made sudden, violent drops; when they would hear the roar of the wind rushing past the transparent nose of the glider and watch the earth recede farther and farther away; when, with eyes transfixed on the glider pilot whose hand tightly gripped the tow-rope release, they would wait to hear the sharp thud as the line was cut and finally know that the attack had actually begun.

It might even be an overstatement to speak of making an "attack" in an engineless, canvas-covered, and unarmed craft, without any parachutes, and with only a single chance to land safely in an area that was teeming with deadly booby traps. The glidermen were well aware that even if there were no problems with their glider, there was always the distinct risk that the C-47 tow plane would be hit by enemy ground or air fire, or would lose power, or would for some reason release the glider and the glidermen aboard to their own fates. Although some generals had taken rides in gliders during training flights in the United States, the glidermen were not informed that no American general had ever flown a glider into combat. Nor could they have known that the first general killed on either side in the Normandy invasion would be an American general killed in the crash landing of a glider.

But that day, the "Day," had not yet arrived and until then the British would continue to be warm and gracious hosts to the glidermen. Many friendships developed with the people of Leicester during the regiment's stay at Scraptoft and a number of American soldiers wedded English brides. The Lord Mayor of Leicester and his wife arranged several functions at which glidermen and other soldiers of the 82nd Airborne were guests, including a large dance at the DeMonfort Hall. Not only Leicester but many other towns and villages in the area also welcomed the American glidermen and other GIs.

4

Men of the 325th Glider Infantry Regiment uncrating ammunition at Camp March Hare, Leicestershire, England, May 1944. (National Archives)

Waiting for Judgment Day

IF ANY RESIDUE of doubt remained in the mind of any gliderman whether the day of reckoning was imminent, that doubt was surely extinguished when it was learned that the chaplain was compiling rosters. Each roster was typed on legal-size paper and was broken down by company. The name of each gliderman was listed in alphabetical order, together with his rank and serial number. There was a column for designating his religious preference and another for the name, address, and relationship of the person who was to be contacted in the event such notification became necessary.

By 26 May plans were almost complete. Then came word of a change that nearly rendered worthless all the orders, overlays, drawings, and plans. The landing zone for the 82nd had been moved from the vicinity of St.-Sauveur-le-Vicomte to a sector closer to the 101st Airborne Division's objectives, between Ste.-Mère Église and Carentan. A mad scramble was begun to revise and reorganize the field orders and overlays and to compile new sets of maps and aerial reconnaissance photos. Orders came down on Sunday, 28 May that it was to be the last day in camp. Both paratroopers and glidermen were ordered to get their equipment into shape and be prepared to pull out the following morning for their respective marshaling areas.

Each gliderman's clothing and equipment consisted of a pair of pants, leggings, and shirt impregnated against gas, a field jacket with a small American flag sewn on the right sleeve, a steel helmet with camouflage net, boots, a gas mask, and a pack. The pack contained a raincoat, a shelter half, a pair of cotton underwear, two pairs of socks, a toothbrush, a mess kit, shaving equipment and towel, chewing gum, boxes of matches, and water-purification tablets. Finally, each gliderman was issued a cartridge belt loaded with armor-piercing ammunition, a bandolier of ammunition, two hand grenades, one smoke grenade, two antitank grenades, an M1 rifle, a bayonet in a scabbard, a trench knife, a first-aid kit with morphine, three K rations, six D rations, and a canteen of water. Glidermen who were part of mortar teams were issued a .45 caliber automatic with ninety rounds of ammunition instead of an M1. Some glidermen were issued Mae West life jackets, which could be inflated either by means of two carbon dioxide cartridges or manually if the cartridges failed or were lost.[1] The sheer weight of the equipment, weapons, and ammunition carried into combat by a gliderman often made it necessary for him to be helped by another man into his glider.

Uncharacteristically, given the grave requirement for secrecy, the airborne camps were not sealed that Sunday night. Hundreds of men went into nearby towns like Leicester for beer and food, and some for a farewell kiss. Even men who had been held in the guardhouse were released to go to the parties. At 10:00 A.M. on Monday, 29 May, the airborne

---

1. Numerous interviews with glidermen confirmed that not all of them were issued these life jackets.

regiments were moved by truck convoy and train from their camps to their new, respective marshaling areas. The marshaling area for the 325th Glider Infantry Regiment was an airfield known as Upottery, approximately fifteen miles northeast of Exeter. Upon arrival, security at the highest level imposed an immediate set of restrictions. The glidermen were

A page from the chaplain's roster of the 325th Glider Infantry Regiment. (Author's Collection)

HEADQUARTERS & HEADQUARTERS COMPANY 2ND BATTALION
325TH GLIDER INFANTRY   *Chap Henry Wall*

Adams, Sidney R.	34254059	Pfc.	(RC)	Annise M. Adams, (Mother)
				1211 Cameron St., Lafayette, La.
Ahart, Francis M.	35717788	Pfc.	P	Myrtle S. Ahart, (Mother)
				Golden Pond, Ky.
Allen, Rufus G.	35657855	Pfc.	C	Albert Allen, (Father)
				Andyville, Ky.
Altman, Herbert M.	35500223	Cpl.	J	Estelle Altman, (Mother)
				11401 Ashbury Ave., Cleveland, Ohio.
Anderson, John R.	35711000	Sgt.	M	Rose Anderson, (Mother)
				Perryville, Ky.
Anderson, Milton W.	36155846	S/Sgt.	P	Mary Anderson, (Mother)
				Shuqualak, Miss.
Arnold, Ed C.	34214001	Pfc.	P	Darlina L. Seymore, (Sister)
				809 Baldwin St., Greenwood, S. C.
Avery, Gordon F.	34550820	Pfc.	P	Fannie B. Avery, (Mother)
				Rt. 1, Hawkinsville, Ga.
Baker, Ivan L.	35513949	Pfc.	P	Muriel Baker, (Mother)
				Box 62, West Mansfield, Ohio.
Bennett, Ester B.	35673064	Cpl.	D	Sarah Bennett, (Mother)
				Cannon, Ky.
Bishop, Gilbert R.	31243762	Pfc.	P	Sarah Bishop, (Mother)
				2627 Hartford Ave., Johnston, R. I.
Boticke, Michael L.	35288903	Sgt.	(RC)	Pauline Boticke, (Mother)
				804 W. Norwood Ave., Youngstown, Ohio.
Boucha, Paul R.	36195027	Pfc.	C	William Boucha, (Father)
				Drummond Isle, Michigan.
Bowen, Luther S.	35157388	Pfc.	P	Louisia Bowen, (Mother)
				Ridgeview, W. Va.
Bowman, Bernard G.	35157170	Pfc.	P	Newton W. Bowman, (Father)
				Alum Creek, W. Va.
Burmeister, Herman E.	36346764	Pfc.	P	Margaret Burmeister, (Mother)
				5821 Palmer St., Chicago, Ill.
Butkus, Alfred A.	15100887	S/Sgt.	C	Mary Ancowien, (Mother)
				RR #2, Box 24, Mantua, Ohio.
Call, Lester L.	35158710	Pfc.	P	Anna Donegan, (Sister)
				718 Indiana Ave., Charleston, W. Va.
Carpenter, Howard A.	36415770	Pfc.	P	Viola Carpenter, (Mother)
				Rt. #1, Newberry, Mich.
Carpenter, James E.	34254587	Pvt.	P	Lula B. Carpenter, (Mother)
				Rt. #2, Sparta, N. C.
Carter, Louie C.	34254908	Sgt.	P	Margaret C. Carter, (Mother)
				P.O. Box 677, China Grove, N. C.
Cassell, Harry L.	33319109	Pfc.	M	Mary W. Cassell, (Mother)
				RFD #1, Nebo, Va.
Chandler, Ernest P.	35157354	Pfc.	P	Hedie Chandler, (Mother)
				Elkview, W. Va.
Clegg, Jim A.	36651105	Pfc.	P	Minnie Clegg, (Mother)
				Rt. #2, Ottawa Lake, Mich.
Cook, Joseph A.	35288994	Sgt.	(RC)	John N. Cook, (Father)
				814 Blakely St., E. Liverpool, Ohio.
Cooper, Robert K.	36596928	Pvt.	P	Freida Cooper, (Mother)
				654 Berry Ave., Chicago, Ill.
Cornely, James C.	35291956	T/5	C	Philizena S. Cornely, (Mother)
				Kirby, Ohio.
Crary, Kenneth J.	36220427	Pvt.	P	Anna Crary, (Mother)
				Rt. #2, Avoca, Wis.
Crede, Harold L.	15100819	Pfc.	P	Lillian M. Crede, (Mother)
				818 N. Broderick St., Delphos, Ohio.
Deaderick, Jr., William F.	34730618	Pvt.	Pfc.	William F. Deaderick, Sr., (Father)
				Gen. Del., Oliver Springs, Tenn.
Dyminski, George J.	36328931	Pvt.	G	Stanley Dyminski, (Father)
				3427 N. Hamlin Ave., Chicago, Ill.
Eccleston, Arthur	35289990	Pfc.	P	Dora Eccleston, (Mother)
				1059 Chestnut St. Ext., E. Liverpool, Ohio.
Elliott, Jack L.	35291852	Pfc.	P	Mollie Elliott, (Mother)
				101 Cleveland Ave., Columbus, Ohio.
England, James A.	35042942	Pfc.	P	Lena P. England, (Mother)
				Lexington, Ky.

- 1 -

prohibited from conversing with anyone outside their own units, even the air corps personnel. After an arduous day of being transported, the men were assigned tents or bunks in hangers. They were ordered to dig foxholes in case of air raids, chowed down about 9:30 P.M., and went to bed.

All movements were limited, including such basics as eating and taking showers. Not only were the men prohibited from communicating with anyone outside of their own unit, but every time they had cause to leave their own area they had to march in formation, under the charge of at least one officer. At the Aldermaston marshaling area, airborne troops found themselves quartered in one half of a huge hanger, which was divided by a large piece of canvas, and they were not allowed to talk to the 101st Airborne men in the other half. Although necessary, the extreme level of security only increased the level of tension that was already reaching the boiling point.

In anticipation of the state of mind that the men would be in prior to the assault and under such tough security measures, efforts were made to diffuse tempers and inject some relaxation. The food they were served was excellent and plentiful and even included ice cream. Movies were regularly scheduled at most of the marshaling areas, and other forms of recreation, such as baseball, were encouraged. At marshaling area Upottery, the 82nd Airborne band entertained the men by playing some of the most popular songs from back home. If the men wanted to simply lie around and sleep, they were allowed to do so. Others read books, the latest issue of *Stars and Stripes,* or letters from home. There was not much reason to write letters because no mail was permitted to leave. For all practical purposes, the men were completely isolated from the rest of the world, which was the intent of the planners.

As the deadline drew nearer, the weather changed from bad to worse; rain and fog overtook the southern part of England. This further restricted the glidermen's already limited activities and often relegated them to the confines of their floorless tents. Scheduled briefing sessions increased in frequency. Lectures were given about the French Resistance, who they were, how they might be located, and what assistance they might be able to furnish. There were discussions about the culture of the French people and the respect that they deserved. Other lectures covered such basics as weapons and equipment, infantry tactics, glider training, and forced landings. Instructions were given on the proper use of rubber life rafts to minimize loss of life in the event a glider was forced to crash into the English Channel, including how to get the raft out of the glider and correctly inflate it.[2] The mortar teams heard lectures that reinforced the fundamentals of operating the 60 mm mortars.

Among the topics that were covered were even such basics as the most advantageous way of exiting a glider. When landing on an airfield, the men had always practiced vacating the gliders and heading for cover off to one side, as opposed to staying in the center of the airstrip and using the glider for cover. This would minimize the opportunity for snipers to zero in on any glidermen attempting to unload the heavy equipment that they had

---

2. A number of glidermen have indicated that they did not recall receiving any instructions regarding rubber life rafts nor were their gliders equipped with them. The evidence suggests that rubber life rafts were aboard most, if not all, the Horsas and possibly not all the Wacos.

Aerial view of American-manned Horsa gliders flanked by C-47s ready for takeoff to Normandy on D-Day. (U.S. Air Force Photo Collection [USAF Neg. No. 53041 AC], courtesy of National Air and Space Museum, Smithsonian Institution)

brought with them, and it would reduce the chance of their being hit by another glider coming in for a landing. During the training exercises held in North Africa, a number of the men witnessed some glidermen who were running down the airfield being struck and killed by another glider that was landing. Glider landings did not enjoy the same precision as those of motorized craft.

The glidermen continued to hear C-47s circling overhead and coming in for landings.

As each day progressed the glidermen saw an enormous gathering of both Waco and Horsa gliders and C-47 towing craft. Row after row of gliders, two abreast, were parked on the runway. The C-47s sat in a single row on either side of them, the nose of each one angled slightly toward the front of the double row of gliders.

As the men sat around and waited, conversations drifted. Some commented sarcastically about how lucky they were to be in an outfit that was going off to engage the enemy in a flying coffin. None of the men, however, were aware of being the subject of a heated debate among certain generals responsible for planning the D-Day invasion. They had no inkling that some casualty estimates of their glider assault had been as high as seventy percent. Nor were the glidermen apprised of the magnitude of danger of the German antiglider devices that had been constructed to oppose them.

General Bradley later explained his position on the risks of the planned assault:

> I conceded that Leigh-Mallory's low-flying C-47s would run into ground fire almost from the moment they made landfall in France. And the Normandy hedgerows would undoubtedly make the glider landing difficult and costly. Both those risks, I asserted, must be subordinated to the importance of Utah Beach and to the prompt capture of Cherbourg. Certainly I would not willingly risk the lives of 17,000 airborne troops if we could accomplish our mission without them. But I would willingly risk them to insure against failure of the invasion. This, in a nutshell, was the issue.[3]

3. Omar N. Bradley, *A Soldier's Story* (New York: Henry Holt, 1951), p. 235.

5

Crossing over Utah Beach into Normandy. Note the underwater obstacles exposed by a low tide. Two other CG-4As being towed by C-47s can be seen at top. (U.S. Air Force Photo Collection [USAF Neg. No. 91812 AC], courtesy of National Air and Space Museum, Smithsonian Institution)

Decision: Normandy

THE PLANNERS RESOLVED that the invasion would take place on the coast near Caen and the Cotentin Peninsula. However, this was hardly a perfunctory determination. Six possible sites were studied and over 800 miles of European coastline were considered in the attempt to find the most advantageous location for the assault. After sifting through the massive amount of available data, they had narrowed their choices to the northern coasts of Holland and Belgium, the mouth of the Seine near Le Havre, the Pas-de-Calais shore, the Brittany peninsula, the Biscay coast as far south as Bordeaux, and the Caen area.

The coasts of Holland and Belgium on the North Sea were far from the airfields in Britain. Since adequate air cover was considered requisite to a successful assault, the great distances that would have had to be overcome eliminated this possibility. Le Havre was appealing because it offered the advantage of being an excellent port. Unfortunately, to attack the mouth of the Seine near Le Havre would have resulted in the Allied forces being split on either side of the river. Besides that, naval guns were defending the sea approaches and the Germans could have easily mounted a counterattack by drawing on the large contingent of troops concentrated at Pas-de-Calais. Le Havre had to be eliminated from consideration.

Brittany had a number of very good ports; however, the majority of them were heavily defended by the enemy and Brittany was also distant—more than 200 miles—from the fighter bases in Britain. Therefore, this area was likewise scrapped because of the importance placed upon air cover. The distance of the Biscay coast almost immediately excluded this area from further consideration. Not only was it well in excess of the range of Allied fighters based in Britain, but the amphibious constituent of the assault would have presented a series of problems. The length of the sea voyage itself most likely would have caused many difficulties, and many of the smaller craft that could be utilized in an assault directly across the Channel would have been inadequate for the voyage to Biscay.

The foregoing analysis reduced the selection down to Pas-de-Calais on the north and the Caen area and Cotentin Peninsula to the south. From the enemy's perspective the most logical focus of an Allied invasion was Pas-de-Calais, astride the narrowest point of the English Channel. Only twenty miles of water separated the cliffs of Dover from the French shore near Calais. Accordingly, the enemy had amassed a large concentration of troops and constructed immense fortifications there. This left the Allied planners with the area between Caen and the Cotentin Peninsula.

The peninsula featured the outstanding deepwater port of Cherbourg, which would be a valuable prize if it could be captured quickly. The Caen area was approximately 200 miles from Paris and 400 miles from the Siegfried Line, making it somewhat removed from the enemy's strong concentration of troops and supplies. From all that could be determined, the beaches were favorable to a seaborne invasion and also led to open country that appeared to offer favorable landing areas for an airborne assault. The river Seine cut off this area of Normandy from the Germans' heavy troop concentration in Pas-de-Calais. Time to secure a lodgment would be critical, and if the bridges over the Seine could be demolished by an air attack, a German counterattack could be inhibited. This chance to increase the time available to the invasion troops by constraining the enemy might prove to be a material benefit of selecting the Caen area.

The planners realized that with the open areas behind the beaches, the airborne assault could play a major role in determining the outcome of the seaborne invasion. If the paratroopers and glidermen could get a foothold inland, they might be able to mount a holding action to block an enemy counterattack against the beaches and open channels for the seaborne invasion forces. With the weapons, ammunition, equipment, and supplies that had been transported in the gliders, the airborne troops could establish a minimal defensive position to stall, if not blunt, a counterattack and afford the invasion forces on the beach sufficient time to move inland. With the bonus of an airborne back up to recommend it, Caen emerged from the foregoing considerations as the best choice.

With the Cotentin Peninsula and the Caen area agreed upon as the objective, the next task was the crystallization of the plan of attack. In December 1943 President Roosevelt informed Gen. Dwight D. Eisenhower that he had been selected at Cairo to become the supreme commander of the Allied Expeditionary Forces in Western Europe. Eisenhower was a logical choice, having been the supreme commander of the Allied Forces in the Mediterranean theater and having recently defeated the Axis armies in North Africa and Sicily. He was known as both a man of great personal charm and a master at the art of compromise, a talent that would serve him well in the position for which he had been singled out.

Field Marshal Montgomery was appointed commander of the 21st Army Group, which was to be the highest land-battle command in the Normandy invasion. Accordingly, Montgomery was to be the commander of all Allied ground forces in the assault on Normandy. The son of a clergyman, Sir Bernard Law Montgomery had been a professional soldier for thirty-five years. Not noted for modesty, his approach to strategy resulted in many conflicts with the other Allied military chiefs. Although often criticized for being overcautious, he was known for his attention to troop morale, careful preparation, detailed planning, and precise execution. Under Montgomery, Lt. Gen. Omar N. Bradley was given command of the American portion of the ground assault, while Lt. Gen. Sir Miles Dempsey was put in command of the British and Canadian land-portion of the assault.

Eisenhower was also to have on his staff Air Chief Marshal Leigh-Mallory, who was given the title of air commander in chief. Like Montgomery, Sir Trafford Leigh-Mallory was the son of a clergyman. He had originally intended to become a lawyer, but with the intervention of World War I his interest turned to being an aviator. After the war he devoted himself to military and aviation problems and worked as both an instructor and a deputy at the British Air Ministry. He accumulated extensive experience in the air and as a military tactician. These attributes, together with a significant amount of combat experience gained in the Battle of Britain, made him the prevailing candidate for the position. He was considered by many to be an ambitious and aggressive commander.

The Americans were assigned to attack on the right, or western, flank of the invasion force. Their assignment was to take two beaches, which were code-named Utah and Omaha. The British and Canadian forces were to take the left side—the eastern flank—and their objectives were the three beaches code-named Gold, Juno, and Sword. This alignment of attack was chosen primarily for reasons of supply. It was anticipated that as soon as the deepwater port of Cherbourg and the other Brittany ports could be secured, the Americans would be supplied directly from the United States. The British, on the other hand, would obtain direct supply routes across the Channel. The ultimate goal was for the British to have access to the Channel ports and Antwerp. Until these ports could be secured, the British would have to rely upon large artificial harbors, known as Mulberries, that were to be constructed.

Bradley felt that an airborne role was essential if the Utah landing was to have any chance of succeeding. He was emphatic in his position that without the support of glidermen and paratroopers, the assault should not be made at all: "Much as I favor the Cotentin assault . . . I would sooner see it go by the boards than risk a landing on Utah without airborne help."[1]

There were two main roads that led from Normandy north into the Cherbourg peninsula. One road ran up the far west coast, while the other ran through Carentan on the east side of the peninsula. The Douve River flowed essentially east and west between these two roads, cutting off the upper two-thirds of the peninsula. The 101st Airborne was delegated to seize hold of the western outlets of the four causeways behind Utah Beach, extending from St.-Germain-de-Varreville to Pouppeville. Next it was to seize the La Barquette lock to the south that controlled the river level and establish bridgeheads across the Douve below Carentan. Then it would open the way for and connect with the seaborne troops assaulting Omaha Beach.

At the same time, the 82nd Airborne was given an even more high-risk assignment. Its objective was to take the west coast road on the peninsula and block the western portion of the neck of the peninsula. Unlike the 101st, the 82nd would be located on the far western side of the peninsula, isolated from the seaborne forces that were to assault Utah. If the 82nd could rapidly assemble into a combat-ready force, it would have a chance of holding out until the Utah Beach assault troops broke through to link up with them.

After a careful analysis of the American airborne plan, Leigh-Mallory very strongly opposed the idea. He felt that the danger the two American airborne divisions would be exposed to was excessive. "I cannot approve your plan," he declared to Bradley. "It is much too hazardous an undertaking. Your losses will be excessive—certainly far more than the gains are worth. I'm sorry, General Bradley, but I cannot go along on it with you."

"Very well, sir," replied Bradley, "if you insist on cutting out the airborne attack, then I must ask that we eliminate the Utah assault. I am not going to land on that beach without making sure we've got the exits behind it."

Montgomery agreed with Leigh-Mallory that the American plan was much too risky and was destined to failure. He added, "If General Bradley insists upon going ahead, he will have to accept full responsibility for the operation. I don't believe it will work."[2]

1. Bradley, *A Soldier's Story,* p. 232.
2. Bradley, *A Soldier's Story,* p. 234.

Leigh-Mallory's extensive experience and detailed scrutiny of the American airborne plan firmly convinced him that the plan was a blueprint for disaster. With the lives of so many glidermen and paratroopers being held in the balance, he went directly to Eisenhower with his concern. Eisenhower recognized that if Leigh-Mallory was right, the entire Utah operation could result in a devastatingly costly failure. Eisenhower, however, was not prepared to refute his air chief's analysis, so he called on Bradley to rebut the disturbing predictions. Bradley confirmed that the use of glidermen and paratroopers was indeed risky, but still insisted that it was absolutely essential to a successful assault on Utah Beach. Eisenhower was left in the untenable position of being confronted with irreconcilable differences between his ground commander and his air chief. After considerable deliberation Eisenhower concurred with Bradley and agreed that the possible benefits of the airborne plan outweighed the massive losses that might be incurred.

Since February, aerial reconnaissance photos had disclosed the existence of an array of vicious-looking German antiglider devices known as Rommelspargel, or "Rommel's Asparagus." These devices were poles, 6–12 inches in diameter and 8–12 feet in length, that were planted 1–2 feet into the ground and 75–100 feet apart. It was the Germans' intention that any gliders that had escaped the antiaircraft fire and that found their way to one of the apparently receptive landing areas would then crash into these poles and be ripped to pieces, killing the glidermen inside. However, the poles by themselves might not have been lethal to the fragile and unarmed incoming gliders. So the poles—some of which were the steel rails from railroad tracks— were wired together and triggered with mines and other explosives. This way not only would the gliders have their wings ripped off and fuselages torn apart, sending them cartwheeling with the glidermen inside, but everyone and everything aboard would be decimated with high explosives.

A wrecked CG-4A glider that crash-landed in one of the numerous fields of "Rommel's Asparagus" near Ste.- Mère-Église on D-Day. (National Archives)

Horsa glider smashes through a roadside hedgerow during the D-Day landing. (National Archives)

German commanders built every antiairborne device they could devise, but the asparagus was their favorite instrument. The extent to which it was used can be judged by Field Marshal Rommel's report after his inspection of the West Wall in the spring of 1944: "The construction of antiparatroop obstacles has made great progress in many divisions. For example, one division alone has erected almost 300,000 stakes, and one corps over 900,000." His report goes on to say, "Erecting stakes alone does not make the obstacles complete; the stakes must be wired together and shells and mines attached to them. The density must be about a thousand stakes per square kilometer. . . . It will still be possible for tethered cattle to pasture underneath these mined obstacles."[3] As implausible as it may seem, the glidermen were not informed of the existence of Rommel's Asparagus during their preassault briefings.

However, the glidermen were to be confronted with another defense even more formidable than Rommelspargel. Almost all of the bocage country of Normandy was divided into small pastures that had been handed down over the centuries from family to family. These divisions were marked by hedgerows, some of them 3–4 feet thick and 3–5 feet high, in which rocks and tree roots intertwined to form a solid mass. Some hedgerows reached the height of a tank. The size of the fields was determined by the perimeter of the hedgerows and often was no more than a few hundred feet in length. These pastures were to serve as the landing fields for the glidermen. Within the brief flash of time that a glider pilot would have for deciding which pasture to land in, he would also have to be dodging trees—many of them fifty feet tall and growing in the hedgerows—to avoid a fatal crash.

3. Gavin, *On to Berlin*, p. 96.

The hedgerows provided not only a lethal natural barrier to the glidermen, but also an excellent defensive fortification for the enemy. Because the hedgerows represented the lines of demarcation between different family plots, each had a small opening to enable a man or perhaps a vehicle to pass through. In an attack, these portals would be guarded by enemy machine guns. Enterprising Germans dug holes through the lower portions of some hedgerows to plant machine-gun nests, giving them an excellent field of fire at ground level over an entire pasture. Also, many hedgerows were backed by deep drainage ditches that the Germans were able to employ as communication trenches. If a glider landed in a field covered by one of these machine-gun emplacements, the glidermen might be slaughtered in their seats before even having a chance to get out of their craft. Under the best of conditions a quick exit would be hindered by the weight of all of the equipment the glidermen were required to carry.

In mid-May the German high command sensed the seriousness of the situation and sent their 91st Infantry Division into the Cotentin Peninsula. With the movement of the German 91st, Allied intelligence confirmed the presence of three German divisions in the peninsula. The location of these divisions was dangerously close to the sector in which the 82nd Airborne was to land. It appeared that the 82nd would be on its own, too far west of Utah Beach to get help from the seaborne troops and vulnerable to being cut off and destroyed by the overwhelming German force.

The gravity of the situation left no other alternative but to make a last-minute change in plans for the 82nd. On 26 May 1944 Maj. Gen. Matthew B. Ridgway, commander of the 82nd Airborne, and his counterpart Gen. Maxwell Taylor, commander of the 101st Airborne, flew to Bristol to recast the attack plans. The new plan that emerged called for the 82nd to land north of the 101st, on both sides of the Merderet River, and within striking distance of Utah Beach. It was to capture the crossroads at Ste.-Mère-Église and guard against possible counterattack from the northwest; seize the areas of Neuville-au-Plain, Chef-du-Pont, Etienville, and Amfreville; then proceed to destroy the bridges over the Douve River and stand ready to advance to the west. The 101st would essentially retain its original mission, except that the 82nd was given the responsibility for seizing the bridges over the Merderet.

Notwithstanding the changes in the plan, Leigh-Mallory was still plagued with the certitude that the American airborne strategy would result in a total catastrophe. A glider/paratroop assault was suspect under the most favorable of conditions, and the new arrangement envisioned the largest, most complex airborne effort that had ever been attempted. The troop-carrier flight plan alone was more elaborate than any that had ever been undertaken, and the number of gliders and aircraft in the operation eclipsed anything that had been tried before

At this time Eisenhower's invasion command post was in Portsmouth. Unknown to Bradley, on 30 May 1944 Leigh-Mallory went to Portsmouth to make a last, personal appeal to Eisenhower to abort the American airborne assault, complaining to him about what he foresaw as "the futile slaughter of two fine divisions."[4] Eisenhower recalls that Leigh-Mallory "believed that the combination of unsuitable landing grounds and anticipated re-

4. Dwight D. Eisenhower, *Crusade in Europe* (New York: Doubleday, 1948), p. 246.

CG-4A gliders come thundering into a partially completed airfield in Normandy, June 1944. (National Archives)

sistance was too great a hazard to overcome."[5] Leigh-Mallory estimated that the Americans would suffer fifty percent casualties among the paratroopers and seventy percent among the glidermen before they ever landed.

Eisenhower was disturbed by the recurrence of a problem that he had assumed was resolved long ago. He went back to his tent alone to reflect upon the question of whether or not to abandon the airborne element of the assault. If he were to agree with Leigh-Mallory and delete the glidermen and paratroopers from the plan, it could mean aborting the entire Utah Beach assault. Bradley had been intractable in his insistence on glidermen and paratroopers for that mission. Eisenhower again found himself having to resolve the irreconcilable viewpoints of his senior ground commander and his chief air commander. If Leigh-Mallory's assessment was correct and the plan went ahead, Eisenhower would bear the responsibility for untold casualties. Leigh-Mallory did not believe that the sector assigned to the British airborne forces contained the same hazards from poor landing sites and extreme enemy resistance that the American sectors had; it was clear that he was not making a blanket objection to an airborne constituent of the assault. His judgment was predicated solely upon his analysis of the American airborne operation.

Finally, later that night, Eisenhower decided the destiny of the American glidermen and paratroopers. He telephoned Leigh-Mallory and told him that the attack was to go ahead as planned. Into that wicked network of antiglider devices and deadly natural defenses the glidermen would go, in their unarmed and engineless gliders, not even suspecting that the chief Allied air commander had predicted that seventy percent of them would be killed, wounded, or injured before having the chance to fight the enemy.

5. Eisenhower, *Crusade in Europe*, p. 246.

Decision: Normandy

6

Beach-landing obstacles exposed by a low tide. (National Archives)

The Enemy Prepares a Reception

ALDERMASTON, RAMSBURY, Greenham Commons, Membury, Welford, Upottery, and Merryfield: These were the names of the airfields, taken from nearby towns and villages, from which the glidermen would take off to spearhead the attack on Hitler's Fortress Europe. Almost 4,000 men, fully laden with their own weapons, ammunition, and supplies, would attack in their gliders. Loaded up with them they would bring the necessities of modern war to the battlefield. They would attempt to glide through the air carrying scores of howitzers, jeeps, trailers, mortars, machine guns, hundreds of tons of ammunition, antitank guns, mines, and grenades, cans of water, medical supplies—virtually everything they could squeeze into their gliders that could be utilized to penetrate the Führer's Atlantic Wall.

On the German side there was no misconception about the coming invasion. The only questions that could not be answered with certainty were how large it would be, when it would occur, and, more importantly, where it would happen. The events transpiring in 1943 culminated in what could only be described as a year of victory for the Allies. Triumphs were achieved in the Atlantic and the Mediterranean. American and British aircraft had commenced the destruction of the German military industrial complex and the battering of the Luftwaffe. On the eastern front entire German armies were slaughtered in Russia. Under the command of von Paulus over 250,000 German soldiers died unnecessarily at Stalingrad alone. The Nazi war machine was bringing about the ineludible ruin of the German state. Since October 1942 Hitler's unchallenged authority had resulted in the destruction of German armies and no one could stop him. Throughout 1943 Nazi losses of men and matériel mounted to staggering proportions.

In April 1941 Field Marshall Karl Rudolf Gerd von Rundstedt was transferred from his position as commander in the west to command Army Group South for the invasion of Russia. From that point on von Rundstedt was aware that the German forces in the west would be deficient to effectively defend the entire western coastline. The gargantuan commitment of forces for the offensive against Russia severely depleted the strength that would be needed to hold the line in the west. The task of defending hundreds of miles of coastline with the resources available was growing almost impossible and the reservoir of men and matériel to draw on was becoming exhausted. The illusion of attaining an impenetrable barrier could not be maintained.

In March 1942 von Rundstedt was reinstated to command Army Group West in France. A pragmatic planner, he knew that the number of divisions at his disposal was insufficient and so he began an intensive analysis of the coastline to ascertain the most probable site for an attempted penetration. If he could not stop an assault, at least he could hope to stall it long enough for fresh reinforcements to be moved in. A student of the brilliant nineteenth-century Prussian general Karl von Clausewitz, von Rundstedt was conscious of the words, "to defend all is to defend nothing."

He deduced that the most inviting target for an Allied assault would be at Pas-de-Calais; not only because it lay the shortest distance across the Channel, but also because it offered the most direct route to the Rhine and into the heart of Germany. The mere twenty miles of water to be crossed offered the opportunity for excellent air cover and reduced the complications for a seaborne force. The fact that Calais was such a conspicuous objective, and thus could be a blind, did not dissuade von Rundstedt in his thinking. He remained steadfast in his conclusion that Calais would be the focal point for the Allied attack.

Notwithstanding von Rundstedt's lucid appraisal, Hitler's intuition was that the Normandy region would be a distinct contender for the site of the invasion. Hitler turned to his best strategist to implement the galvanization of the Atlantic Wall. In November 1943 Field Marshall Erwin Rommel was appointed, under the command of von Rundstedt, to take charge of the inspection and strengthening of the coastal fortifications. Rommel was an outstanding field commander with exceptional experience, and he was admired by the German people and respected by his Allied opponents for his string of spectacular successes. World War I provided him with a distinguished infantry career and at the outbreak of World War II Hitler made him commander of his personal headquarters. He quickly made a name for himself as the consummate armored strategist in North Africa and in June 1942 was made a field marshal. In Germany he was elevated to hero status, a position that was encouraged by Hitler, who perceived no political aspirations in him.

In January 1944 Rommel accepted full command of Army Group B, which was charged with defending France from the expected Allied invasion. He shared Hitler's view that the Normandy area would be the objective for the Allied assault troops and he maintained that the invaders must be annihilated while still at sea or, as a last resort, on the beaches. He wanted the armored divisions close by and available to him so that he could deliver a rapid and massive counterattack to overwhelm the invasion forces. His experience in North Africa, moreover, had taught him what an intolerable risk it was to attempt to move armored columns in daylight under the bombsights of enemy aircraft. The Allied air threat loomed over every decision needing to be made. He believed that if his Panzers were not near the Allied assault positions, the tank divisions would most likely never get there in time to dispense the counterstrike required.

However, irreconcilable strategies arose between Rommel, on the one hand, and von Rundstedt and the Panzer generals, on the other. The latter disagreed with Rommel's opinion that Normandy would be the site for the primary Allied thrust. Also von Rundstedt wanted to unleash massive counterattacks upon the invaders after they had broken through the coastal sea-defense network—an idea that was diametrically opposed to Rommel's. Moreover, von Rundstedt agreed that Allied air supremacy would make it difficult to successfully move the tank divisions; but if the armor were situated nearer to Normandy and the invasion did take place at Calais, the tank columns could find themselves trapped and eliminated, unable to assist in the defense of Calais.

In February and again at the end of April 1944, Rommel issued the following directive to his army commanders: "In the short time left before the great offensive starts, we must succeed in bringing all defenses to such a standard that they will hold up against the strongest attacks. Never in history was there a defense of such an extent with such an obstacle as the sea. The enemy must be annihilated before he reaches our main battlefield. We must stop him in the water, not only delaying him but destroying all his equipment while it is still afloat."[1]

Rommel remained convinced that Normandy was the sector where he should concentrate his defenses and that it was essential to deprive the enemy of gaining a foothold ashore. The Allies would have to be dealt such a severe blow that they would lose the ability to mount a second attack. Hitler likewise continued to hold to his hunch that Normandy, with its excellent port at Cherbourg, was the key Allied objective. His intelligence reports on Allied troop activity and concentrations in the southern region of England only buttressed this judgment. Still, the logic of von Rundstedt was not to be capriciously disregarded. If Pas-de-Calais were not the principle target, it could be part of the Allied design for a secondary assault. This possibility continued to bedevil Hitler.

Meanwhile, Rommel attacked the assignment given to him with the same vigor and skill that he was known for on the battlefield. From Denmark to Spain, over 800 miles of coastline had to be defended and fortified. He devised his defenses with the idea of forming a thin, hard crust along the beaches that would be backed up with infantry divisions a short distance behind. These divisions could be called upon, subject to their varying degrees of maneuverability, to counterattack against any determined landings. Although the Atlantic Wall itself could not stop a massive concentrated assault, it could slow down an invading force. By accomplishing a delaying action, Rommel would have time to bring in reinforcements.

Indeed, buying time for reserves to arrive was the ultimate function of the Wall. If he could bloody the Allied invading force and possibly even divide it, Rommel might gain sufficient time to muster a formidable counterstrike with his reserves. When used in a blocking technique, a fixed defensive line of heavy concrete fortifications could be worth the temporary equivalent of a number of divisions of men. However, fixed fortifications, no matter how well designed and constructed, would be rendered useless without the addition of mobile reserves. It was, after all, the lack of mobile reserves that had doomed the mighty and "impregnable" Maginot Line.

Rommel set about increasing the number of his casemated guns and ordered the pouring of massive amounts of concrete. Many thousands of booby-trapped beach obstacles were constructed in an elaborate network of devices designed to rip open the bottoms of landing craft, even the flat-bottomed craft used in beach landings. He reiterated to his commanders that the first twenty-four hours would be decisive; there would be no second chances. "If we do not stop the invasion and do not drive the enemy back into the sea, the war will be lost".[2] Some 6,000,000 mines were laid.

After the water obstacles the invading forces would be confronted with a plethora of beach impediments. Rommel personally supervised the creation and installation of thousands of hedgehogs, antitank obstacles, pointed logs, mined stakes angled toward the sea, and immense steel creations, known as Tetrahydra and Belgian Gates. Whenever possible, the obstructions were decorated with mines and barbed wire. Behind the beach portion

1. R. W. Thompson, *D-Day: Spearhead of Invasion* (New York: Ballantine, 1968), p. 60.

2. Thompson, *D-Day: Spearhead of Invasion,* p. 59.

of the crust were the firepower units of the Wall: mortar emplacements and reinforced concrete pillboxes that could spray the beaches with machine-gun fire; concrete bunkers harboring antitank guns and casemated artillery guns; and behind them, even heavier coastal artillery guns with sufficient firepower to destroy invading ships, and more mortars sighted on the fields where gliders might land.

Rommel utilized virtually every device and scheme imaginable to crush the invasion. If there were penetration through the beach defenses, the battle hardened soldiers of the Wehrmacht and the Panzer divisions would be rushed in. To stop the glidermen and paratroopers, fields were flooded beyond the beaches to drown the men who would be loaded down with their heavy equipment. Other glidermen would drown before they could vacate their sinking gliders. For the glidermen especially Rommel prepared his namesake weapon, the Rommelspargel—the extensive system of poles that were planted in the ground to tear the gliders to pieces. Under Rommel's personal charge the installation of these fiendish devices ran into the hundreds of thousands, along with the thousands of mines and other explosive charges that were carefully wired to the poles.

The 5, 6, and 7 June were selected by the Allies as the most appropriate days for the invasion. There would be a full moon to light the way for the glidermen and paratroopers and there would be low morning tides to assist the seaborne landings. But in the first days of June the weather took an abrupt turn for the worse. The intensity of the unexpected storm forced Eisenhower to make a crucial decision. His first choice was to proceed with the invasion as planned. This entailed risking the airborne force in a torrential storm, as well as the small landing craft that could be sunk by the heavy sea. If postponement were the decision, all the timetables could be disrupted and there was no guarantee the weather would improve anyway.

On Sunday morning, 4 June, Eisenhower met with his commanders at Portsmouth to discuss the weather conditions. D-Day had been scheduled for the next day. Unanimity did not prevail. Although Generals Montgomery and Walter Bedell Smith were not in favor of a postponement, Leigh-Mallory contended that the operation must be delayed. Air Chief Marshall Tedder was not sure. Eisenhower decided against adding the hazard of violent weather to an already extraordinarily dangerous venture. The airborne element was too fundamental a component of the overall operation. Leigh-Mallory's warnings of seventy percent casualties among the American glidermen was an admonition that could not be discounted.

German weather stations were likewise following the storm and came to the same conclusions as the Allied weather forecasters. The indications portended the worst storm in twenty years and unfavorable weather that could last a week. Rommel also weighed the situation. The Allies would not be foolhardy enough to attempt an invasion in the middle of a tempest, he reasoned, and undertaking a glider assault in the midst of a turbulent storm would be beyond comprehension. Rommel discussed the conditions with his commanders including Admiral Krancke and General Blumentritt, who had also considered the data received from their meteorological experts. All concurred that heavy rains, gale winds, and a churning sea would deprive the enemy of the opportunity for invasion. The storm was moving inland with all its fury toward southern England, so it seemed that all would be well for at least another week.

However, German weather forecasters were not privy to all the information that the Allied meteorologists had. Allied weather stations far out in the North Atlantic and in Greenland were transmitting data back to England that suggested there was a possibility that the storm front would lift for a twenty-four hour period on Tuesday, 6 June.

Exhausted from the grueling schedule of work that he exacted from himself and secure in the knowledge of what his weather forecasters were predicting, Rommel left on the morning of 5 June for his home at Ulm on the Danube for a few days of rest. He planned on paying a visit to Hitler to discuss the posture of defense strategies and intended also to see his son Manfried and perhaps a few relatives and close friends. He looked forward to celebrating the birthday of his wife, Lucie Marie, on 6 June.

Meanwhile, the Führer was staying at his opulent retreat in the mountains with his mistress, Eva Braun. He planned on taking advantage of the day by accepting only a light schedule, consisting of two meetings to be held with his staff. He intended to spend the evening listening to the melodic tones of the German composer Wagner.

7

Three American glidermen walk beneath a canopy of waiting Horsa gliders as they await the go-ahead for takeoff to Normandy on D-Day. (U.S. Air Force Photo Collection [USAF Neg. No. 53244 AC], courtesy of National Air and Space Museum, Smithsonian Institution)

From Chicago to Hackensack: The Final Plan

THE GLIDER ASSAULT PLAN was, by any standard, remarkable in its degree of detail and complexity. Glidermen from the 82nd and 101st Airborne Divisions were to attack in a precisely timed sequence of six separate glider missions. The 82nd Airborne, with the battle-hardened glidermen of the 325th Glider Infantry Regiment, would bear the burden of four of the missions, while the Screaming Eagles of the 101st Airborne would strike with the other two. The six glider missions were code-named Chicago, Detroit, Keokuk, Elmira, Galveston, and Hackensack.

The enormous job of towing the American glider force of 513 gliders into Normandy was charged to the 9th Troop Carrier Command, which had bases throughout southern England. A total of seven troop carrier groups would be required to tow the massive glider armada. Five of the assignments were given to the 434th, 435th, 436th, 437th, and 438th groups, which formed the 53rd Troop Carrier Wing. The remaining missions were given to the 439th and 441st groups, both under the command of the 50th Troop Carrier Wing.

A typical American troop carrier group consisted of fifty-two planes, which was broken down into a headquarters unit having four aircraft and four squadrons having a dozen planes each. The groups underwent intensive practice with both Wacos and Horsas. Sometimes the training involved towing two Wacos at one time, which a C-47 was quite capable of accomplishing. However, the weight of a large, loaded Horsa would not permit double towing, so those flights were limited to single tows. It was decided later that all glider attacks into Normandy would be restricted to one glider per tow plane.

Mission Chicago was to be the first glider assault and was scheduled to take off just after 1:00 A.M., 6 June, from Aldermaston in Berkshire. A serial of fifty-three Wacos would be towed by C-47s of the 434th Troop Carrier Group. The glider mission would be under the command of Brig. Gen. Donald Pratt, assistant division commander of the 101st. Pratt would fly in the lead glider known as the Fighting Falcon. One hundred fifty-five glidermen of the 327th Glider Infantry Regiment would squeeze into their gliders, along with all the firepower they could cram in: sixteen 57 mm antitank guns, two and a half tons of ammunition, twenty-five jeeps, medical supplies, and eleven tons of other equipment such as antitank mines and grenades, and cans of water. Their target was designated LZE—landing zone east. Scheduled arrival time was just after 4:00 A.M. By design the gliders were to land under cover of darkness to minimize the chances of being raked by German antiaircraft fire; however, attempting to land in the dark in hedgerow country that was studded with Rommel's Asparagus entailed a deadly risk.

Glidermen of the 82nd Airborne took responsibility for Mission Detroit. Detroit would also take off just after 1:00 A.M., 6 June, from Ramsbury in Wilts. A serial of fifty-two C-47s of the 437th Troop Carrier Group would tow an equal number of Wacos in the dark-

Double glider tow. Six CG-4A gliders are being towed in formation by three C-47s. (U.S. Air Force Photo Collection [USAF Neg. No. A 82561 AC], courtesy of National Air and Space Museum, Smithsonian Institution)

ness of the early morning hours. The timetable called for the first glider in Mission Detroit to leave the ground about ten minutes after the first Chicago glider became airborne. The target was farther to the west, designated LZW. Arrival time in enemy territory was also to be under cover of darkness, just after 4:00 A.M. Two hundred twenty fully equipped, combat-ready glidermen were to climb into their gliders with as much combat equipment as they could manage to fit in to the tight space: sixteen 57 mm antitank guns, ammunition, twenty-two jeeps, five trailers, cans of water, medical supplies, and ten more tons of miscellaneous equipment.

Keokuk, named after the small city in southeast Iowa on the Mississippi, was to be the smallest of the six missions in numbers of gliders and the first daylight mission. Thirty-two Horsas towed by C-47s of the 434th Troop Carrier Group would make up the serial that was scheduled to lift off from Aldermaston at 6:30 P.M. Keokuk was to be the final Normandy mission of the glidermen of the 101st. Besides packing in 157 fully loaded glidermen and medical and staff personnel into the huge Horsas, the gliders would carry forty vehicles, six howitzers, medical supplies, water, and nineteen tons of other equipment. It would be the first mission comprised solely of the big, unwieldy wooden Horsas, or as they were called by the glidermen, "English coffins." Planned time of arrival behind enemy lines at target LZE was around 9:00 P.M.

Glidermen of the 82nd would also undertake the most prodigious glider assault of them all, Mission Elmira. A total of 176 heavily packed gliders, lifting off from four airfields, would attempt a synchronized attack. The rapid loading of men and matériel, the prompt attainment of tolerable load balances aboard each glider, together with a successful hook-up procedure with each C-47, presented great logistical problems of coordination and precision timing. The days and weeks of redundant training would be severely tested. The 82nd's target for Elmira was LZW, where it would link up with the glidermen of Mission Detroit and the other paratroopers of the 82nd.

Because of its size Elmira would be divided into two echelons, with each of them being further subdivided into two serials. It was to be the first glider mission to employ both Horsas and Wacos together, which would present its own set of problems. The towing speed of the Waco being faster than that of the lumbering Horsa, the two gliders could not fly in the same formation. The decision to divide Elmira was also driven by the concern with having too many gliders attempting to land at the same time. Each glider would have only one landing opportunity, with no second go-around. Additionally, smaller glider trains would afford greater fighter protection on the way over the Channel and into enemy territory.

The first echelon would be made up of two serials consisting of twenty-six and fifty gliders, respectively. The first serial would be comprised of eight Wacos and eighteen Horsas and would be towed by twenty-six C-47s of the 437th Troop Carrier Group. Takeoff would occur from Ramsbury at approximately 6:40 P.M., about ten minutes after the first

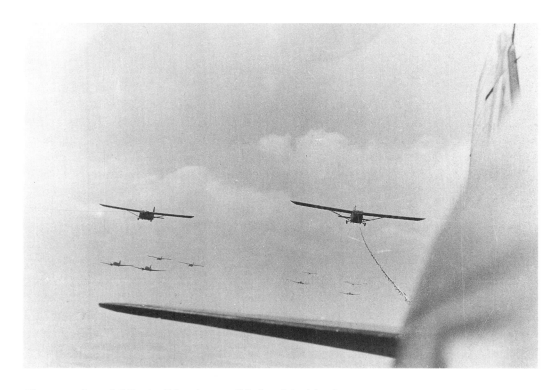

Close-up view of CG-4A gliders in tow. (National Archives)

glider teams of Keokuk left the field. The second serial would be made up of fourteen Wacos and thirty-six Horsas and would be towed into combat by the 438th Troop Carrier Group from Greenham Commons in Berkshire at about 6:50 P.M. The timetable called for landing behind enemy lines in LZW at 9:00 P.M. Sixty-four vehicles, most of them jeeps, would be lashed down aboard the gliders, together with thirteen 57 mm antitank guns, ammunition, medical supplies, twenty-four tons of additional equipment, and 437 men weighted down with their tools of war.

Elmira's second echelon would be formed by two fifty-glider serials. Departure would be about two hours after the first echelon. The first serial would contain two Wacos and forty-eight Horsas, which were to be towed by the 436th Troop Carrier Group from Membury in Berkshire. The use of the huge Horsas would enable the glidermen to take a greater size and weight of firepower to the enemy than could be carried by the Wacos alone. Four hundred eighteen glidermen, mostly from the 319th Glider Field Artillery Battalion, together with some medical personnel and engineers, comprised the human cargo. Into their gliders would go twelve 75 mm pack howitzers, twenty-six tons of ammunition, thirty-one jeeps, plus twenty-five more tons of combat equipment.

The second serial of the second echelon would consist of twelve Wacos and thirty-eight Horsas towed by fifty C-47s of the 435th Troop Carrier Group from the airfield at Welford in Berkshire. Three hundred nineteen artillerymen of the 320th Field Artillery Battalion, 82nd Airborne would commit the heaviest gliderborne artillery to the D-Day fight. They would bring twelve 105 mm howitzers, thirty-three tons of ammunition, twenty-eight jeeps, medical supplies, water, and twenty-three tons of additional matériel. Any of these heavier guns that reached their designated landing zones would contribute immeasurably to the Allies' fighting capability. With Mission Elmira the glidermen of the 82nd Airborne would complete the last American glider assault undertaken on D-Day.

Missions Galveston and Hackensack would immediately commence in the early hours of D plus one, delivering the most potent gliderborne fighting force yet. The entire 325th Glider Infantry Regiment, veterans of Italy and North Africa, would attack the Wehrmacht behind the Atlantic Wall. Under the command of Col. Harry L. Lewis, the 325th would enter the fray prepared to execute any combat mission ordered by General Ridgway, commander of the 82nd. Landing was targeted for LZE. Galveston would have one hundred gliders, divided into two serials. Takeoff for the serials was scheduled for 4:30 A.M.

Serial one would leave from Ramsbury and would consist of thirty-two Wacos and eighteen Horsas towed by fifty C-47s from the 437th Troop Carrier Group. The 1st Battalion of the 325th and some glidermen from an engineering company—some 717 heavily laden, combat-ready glidermen in all—would climb into the gliders. Although the weight of so many glidermen with all their weapons and personal equipment would limit the amount of additional matériel that could be airlifted, the gliders would still be able to carry seventeen vehicles, nine howitzers, and another twenty tons of combat equipment.

Serial two of Galveston was to depart from Aldermaston with fifty Wacos towed by the 434th Troop Carrier Group. This serial would carry eleven howitzers, five tons of ammunition, twenty-four vehicles, and one and a half tons of equipment and supplies. Climbing on board would be glidermen from the headquarters of the 325th, the reconnaissance platoon of the 82nd Airborne, and some additional artillerymen and engineers, for a total force of 251 men. Both serials were scheduled to arrive on the battlefield at 7:00 A.M. and together would deliver almost 1,000 glidermen behind enemy lines.

Mission Hackensack was to be the final American glider attack in Normandy. It would consist of two serials of fifty gliders each. The landing objective for Hackensack would be LZW. Takeoff for the first serial was scheduled for 6:30 A.M., two hours after Galveston had begun, from Upottery in Devon. Twenty Wacos and thirty Horsas would be towed by the 439th Troop Carrier Group. From Upottery the 2nd Battalions of both the 325th and 401st Glider Infantry Regiments would board their gliders. The 2nd Battalion of the 401st had been attached to the 325th as its third battalion to give the regiment a full complement of three combat-ready battalions of glidermen. Serial one contained an aggregate fighting force of 968 glidermen who would crowd aboard with eleven tons of ammunition, five vehicles, and ten tons of other supplies, including mines, antitank grenades, mortars, medical equipment, and water.

The second serial of Hackensack was timed to take off just after 7:00 A.M. from Merryfield in Somerset. Fifty Wacos would be towed aloft by the 441st Troop Carrier Group. This serial would carry more equipment and less men than the first serial. Three hundred sixty-three glidermen, mostly service personnel of the 325th and the 401st, would board their Wacos with thirteen 81 mm mortars, six tons of ammunition, twenty jeeps, nine trailers, and eighteen tons of miscellaneous combat equipment, including mines and antitank grenades.

Given the enormous number of planes and gliders involved, the exactitude the timetables called for, and the demands that would be placed on all the participants, there was virtually no margin for error in these plans. All the gliders would have to be airborne by their appointed times, flying formations maintained, and critical flight paths followed. The glider formations were supposed to be routed to France directly over the Allied naval armada. If the Luftwaffe happened to make an appearance, the glider force might be mistaken for enemy aircraft and in the tension of the moment could be fired upon by naval antiaircraft guns.

To address the concern over this grave danger to the airborne forces, members of the troop carrier command held a meeting in early May with the commander in chief of the Allied Expeditionary Naval Forces, Adm. Sir Bertram Ramsay. Ramsay appreciated the magnitude of the airborne assault and the key role it was to play in the overall D-Day plan. On the other hand, he had to consider the risks to the ships of the navies under his command as the Allied naval commander in chief. He knew that his forces might indeed be unable to distinguish friend from foe among all the aerial activity overhead. He also knew that Leigh-Mallory, the air commander in chief and a fellow countryman, was predicting that only thirty percent of the American glidermen would survive the ordeal of getting to the battlefield.

Ramsay had been in most of the meetings where the issue of the glidermen had been the topic of heated debate. It was almost certain that Bradley would appeal to Eisenhower to abandon the Utah assault if his seaborne force were denied the airborne support. Ramsay remembered that Montgomery had concurred with Leigh-Mallory's conclusion that the American glidermen were being sent to their slaughter. He also recalled a discussion in which it was brought out that the glidermen were not being issued parachutes, while even

CG-4A gliders crossing the English Channel on their way to Normandy to participate in the initial assault behind enemy lines on D-Day. Naval units can be seen below. (U.S. Air Force Photo Collection [USAF Neg. No. 51600 AC], courtesy of National Air and Space Museum, Smithsonian Institution)

the men in the tow planes were. Could he, Ramsay, be party to compounding the probable carnage of the glidermen by making them run the gauntlet of concentrated firepower from the largest naval armada ever assembled? Yet if he instructed his ships not to fire on any approaching aircraft, he would be disarming his navy and the navies of the other countries under his command. Such an act would perhaps be an invitation to disaster.

Nevertheless, Ramsay's comprehension of the vital importance of the airborne element brought him to a most singular decision. He agreed to order a prohibition on all naval antiaircraft fire at the times that airborne missions were scheduled to fly over his ships. To further decrease the likelihood of mistaking Allied aircraft for German planes, the 9th Troop Carrier Command decided to apply a special marking to each plane and glider. The final design selected was comprised of three white stripes alternating with two black stripes, each stripe being two feet wide, which would be painted from front to back on each wing and around the fuselage toward the rear. Due to the obvious need for security, the order to paint the design on the gliders and planes was not given until 4 June, at which time hundreds of men moved hurriedly to complete the job for D-Day.

It was apparent to almost anyone that the CG-4A Waco glider was devoid of any degree of crash protection. Survivability of pilot and glidermen would depend upon its landing without impacting any natural or man-made obstacles on the ground. In training flights the landing fields offered open areas that were free from any dangerous impedi-

American-manned Horsa gliders and C-47s ready for takeoff to Normandy on D-Day. Note the striped markings that clearly identify them as Allied. (Silent Wings Museum)

ments. These practice landing fields, however, did not in any way duplicate the types of terrain that were likely to be encountered in combat missions.

The mandate to the glider designers had not specifically required that the structural integrity of the CG-4A be capable of tolerating a direct frontal impact; forward crash survivability was not a prerequisite for operational use. Although it might seem that the lack of such a requirement was tantamount to gross negligence, it was in fact the product of conventional aircraft design mentality. Aircraft had never been thought of as armored vehicles. Any unnecessary addition of weight was anathema to aircraft performance and speed. The added protection afforded by armor that was built into a fighter or bomber was always counterbalanced by a concomitant loss of airworthiness. Therefore, judgments of the extent to which armor protection should be provided were based upon calculations of survivability from enemy gunfire, given the caliber of air-to-air and ground-to-air fire that was likely to be encountered.

Compromises were made by the designers of each aircraft that would allow it to sustain a modicum of direct low-caliber hits in nonvital areas without being destroyed. Ideally, the plane should still be able to fulfill its mission and return to its home base for a landing. Under the most favorable circumstances, the return would not only preserve the lives of the pilot and crew, but would also allow the plane to be repaired. This expectation was predicated upon the assumption that the plane would retain sufficient maneuverability to

From Chicago to Hackensack: The Final Plan

CG-4A glider equipped with the Griswold Nose crash protection system. The ski-like device known as the Corey Skid, which can be seen at the bottom of the fuselage, was designed to deflect small obstacles. (Silent Wings Museum)

circle the field if necessary and make one or more approaches before landing. Hence, there never was any great emphasis given to survivability from the front-end crash of a fighter or bomber, which could usually effect a safe landing on the second attempt, if it could not do so on the first.

When this design philosophy was adopted by the glider designers, the critical hypothesis that had allowed airplane designers to compromise between armor and maneuverability broke down. As a class of aircraft the glider was deprived of any second chances for landing. A glider that was not in proper alignment for its approach would not have the engine power to ascend, circle, and try again; there was no engine. It was like a brick with wings, unable to avoid any ground obstacle or antiglider device that was detected at the last minute. Although not building in front-end crash protection stemmed from conventional aircraft design reasoning, a combat glider was not a conventional aircraft, and the initial failure to include such basic protection was an unfortunate commentary on the state of glider-design thinking.

Restored frame of the nose section of a CG-4A glider equipped with a Griswold Nose crash protection system and a Corey Skid. (Author's Collection)

The flaw in this reasoning was finally recognized by the army, which acknowledged that gliders needed some form of front-end protection. In mid-1943 the Ludington-Griswold Company of Saybrook, Connecticut, submitted plans for such a system for the CG-4A. The design called for a rugged structure that would absorb the shock of crashes with small trees, fences, wooden stakes, and other similar obstacles. The system was devised to automatically collapse, deflecting small objects and thereby minimizing casualties. The army agreed that the device would minimize loss of life and injury to the glidermen, but held that it would be too costly. They instructed Ludington-Griswold to abandon the proposed system and deliver a modified design. The new design basically consisted of only the interior tubular framework of the original crash protection system. The structure, which came to be known as the Griswold Nose, could be assembled and bolted onto the front of the Waco.

In April 1944 the work of adding Griswold Noses to those Wacos destined for D-Day commenced. As each day passed and assemblies were completed, it became obvious that the job of modifying all of the Normandy-bound Wacos would not be finished in time. Adherence to priorities and timetables took over. Installation of the protective nose systems completely stopped a week before D-Day, leaving many of the Wacos and their glidermen without any crash safety protection for the invasion.

8

Moments before takeoff for Normandy: going to war in a canvas-covered glider.
(Silent Wings Museum)

The Glider Assault on Normandy

THE GLIDERMEN ON ALL AIRFIELDS convened for final briefings of their missions. Every man was fully apprised of all aspects of his unit's plans. The details given were not only for D-Day but for the days following. In the event the officers were killed, any surviving noncoms could assume command and continue to fight on. Unlike some other outfits, in airborne units officers commanded from the front with their men.

Maps showing the specific landing targets as well as the locations of all roads and bridges were carefully studied. Information regarding the terrain, sites where linkups were to occur, and the names of local villages were committed to memory. Likewise, passwords were memorized and toy "crickets" were issued to each man to assist in distinguishing friend from foe, one click of the cricket being the challenge and two clicks the proper countersign. All equipment and weapons were checked and rechecked repeatedly. Each man was issued 200 francs of invasion money, which was equivalent to about four U.S. dollars. Everyone was ordered to tape his dog tags together to prevent them from making even the slightest noise, and everyone stuffed toilet paper into his mess kit to keep it from clattering.

For some of them the meal they were about to eat would be their last supper. Like the condemned, the glidermen were given a hot and substantial dinner. Tension was high but there seemed to be a subdued, yet general feeling of confidence. Some of the men became quiet. After long, hot showers they donned two-piece long underwear and socks. Having to wear long underwear in June gave everybody something to complain about, but there was a method to the madness. The gliderman's uniform consisted of olive drab woolen shirt and pants that had been impregnated with an antigas agent, which caused the uniform to become stiff, greasy, and cold. The underwear protected the man's bare skin from coming into direct contact with his uniform. Over this layer went impregnated canvas leggings and a field jacket with an American flag sewn on the right arm. Boots and a steel helmet with camouflage net completed the basic combat uniform.

Fully dressed, with equipment and weapons at the ready, some men dozed, some spoke in hushed whispers, some prayed. None would get a night's sleep. At 10:00 P.M., 5 June, the shriek of a whistle followed by two more shattered the silence of the airfield at Aldermaston, signaling the beginning of the most celebrated glider assault in world history. Everyone got up and formed up into the lines at the latrine and the mess tent. The chow line moved rapidly as the men were dished out a hasty breakfast of ham and eggs, then went back to the tents to quickly secure all their gear. Thirty minutes had passed since the first whistle.

Each company formed up by platoon, and each platoon was checked by squad. All glidermen were accounted for, all weapons and equipment okayed. Each man looked over the equipment of the man in front of him: an M1 weighing more than eight and a half pounds, or an even heavier BAR, the air-cooled, fully automatic rifle capable of firing 200 to 350 rounds per minute; a fully loaded cartridge belt and two bandoliers of ammuni-

Invasion money
issued to glidermen.
(Author's Collection)

tion—one extra bandolier per man; and most likely an extra grenade. Altogether over seventy pounds of weapons, ammunition, and equipment was hung on the shoulders, slung over the back, stuffed into the pack, and crammed into the pockets of each man.

When the order was given the glidermen moved out to the airstrip where the C-47s and their gliders were lined up. The glidermen had been to the airstrip a few days before and most of them had in fact helped to lay the steel runway that they were about to take off from. For days convoys of trucks had delivered loads of steel panels with a kind of corrugated structure to some airfield sites. The troop carrier groups had laid out the best location for a runway and put the panels together in an interlocking grid pattern that was sturdy and neat. The steel runway produced a smoother takeoff for the tow plane and glider combination, thereby minimizing the chance of a mishap, and reduced the amount of power that would otherwise be needed to tow the glider over a bumpy, grass-covered field.

The glidermen were broken out into groups and marched to their gliders. Often a gliderman would have to give a boost to help the heavily loaded man in front of him get aboard. The men climbed over and around boxes of mines, cans of water, and cases of ammunition and mortar shells that were lashed down to the floor of the glider. Balancing the load had to be achieved no matter how crowded the men were or how difficult the cargo

Prefabricated
steel runway.
(Jack L. Innes)

would make an emergency escape. Seat belts were strapped on and helmets were secured. They could hear the first coughs and sputters of the Pratt and Whitney twin engines turning over. At exactly 1:19 A.M., 6 June, the first C-47 of Mission Chicago thundered down the steel runway at Aldermaston, towing the Fighting Falcon with Gen. Don Pratt in the copilot's seat.

C-47 on a runway waiting for glider hookup. (Silent Wings Museum)

The moon was bright and the tow planes and gliders accomplished smooth takeoffs and promptly assembled into columns of four. Everything appeared to be going well until one of the Wacos suddenly broke loose, landing just four miles from its point of departure. Unfortunately this was the glider that carried the 101st Airborne's powerful SCR-499 radio, which was supposed to be used to communicate with headquarters regarding the mission's progress and the enemy's positions and strength.

Crossing the peninsula the glider train encountered enemy ground fire. One plane was quickly shot down. Bullets tore through a glider, stitching the canvas walls with machine-gun fire and sending it careening into the ground. The ground fire intensified, causing a slight separation in the formation but not enough to deter the gliders from continuing their attack. One tow pilot became disoriented and released a helpless glider near the town of Carentan, eight miles south of the landing zone. Seven more C-47s and twenty-two Wacos took hits.

At 3:54 A.M., a full six minutes ahead of schedule, the lead glider cut away from its tow plane to search in the dark for a landing area. The cutoff altitude was only 450 feet. With almost no light and only seconds to try to locate safe patches of earth, the gliders descended into German-held territory. All of a sudden the deadly hedgerows, the fifty-foot-high trees, and the rooftops of farmhouses became terrifyingly visible. The glidermen clutched their rifles and anything else they could find to hold on to as they began crash-landing. Numerous gliders smashed into trees, hedgerows, and ditches. Wings were cleaved off, sending the remaining fuselages with their glidermen tumbling out of control.

Six gliders of Mission Chicago actually landed in the designated LZ. Fifteen others, surprisingly, managed to land within only half a mile of it and another ten near the village of Les Forges, about a mile away. Another eighteen were strewn all over to the south and southeast of the target and all but one were within two miles of the LZ.

Despite all the crash landings, Mission Chicago casualties were relatively light. General Pratt died when his glider collided with a tree-studded hedgerow. Four other glidermen were killed, seventeen were severely injured, and seven more were missing and were presumed to have been captured. Almost all the gliders were wrecked and unsalvageable. Sniper fire and mortar shells peppered some of the survivors as they tried to extricate themselves and their equipment from their crashed gliders. However, they retrieved from the wreckage six of the 57 mm antitank guns, three jeeps, and some of the ammunition and other supplies. The glidermen also were able to keep their wits about them and assemble into their units to become an effective fighting force.

Also at 10:00 P.M., 5 June, the whistles blew at Ramsbury to muster the glidermen of the 82nd Airborne. Their Mission Detroit was scheduled to land in enemy territory at precisely 4:10 A.M., just ten minutes after the first Mission Chicago gliders had landed. At 1:29 A.M., 6 June, the first C-47 roared down the steel runway at Ramsbury. Loading and takeoff procedures were exemplary and the entire serial of fifty two tow planes and their gliders was airborne by 1:53 A.M.—one successful takeoff approximately every thirty seconds.

Visibility was ten miles and the weather over the Channel was good. Then, as the airborne armada approached Normandy, the tow planes hit a dense cloud bank and seven gliders were accidentally released. The clouds were so thick that the glider pilots could not see their tugs. Antiaircraft fire started to rake the sky train. The C-47s descended to 500 feet but still found visibility to be poor. Seven more gliders were prematurely released over the flooded fields west of the Merderet River. Some had their tow ropes split by enemy bullets.

Glidermen of Neptune

Fully loaded CG-4A gliders lined up on runway awaiting their turn for takeoff to Normandy on D-Day. Note that glider number one's tail is up and the tow rope is taut. (U.S. Air Force Photo Collection [USAF Neg. No. 83087 AC], courtesy of National Air and Space Museum, Smithsonian Institution)

Glider attack over Normandy on D-Day. American gliders cut loose from tow planes and circle to find a landing site in "postage-stamp" size fields. (Imperial War Museum, London)

As it turned out, the clouds were more of a blessing than a curse for Detroit. As soon as the glider combinations got through the cloud cover, they were barraged by heavy antiaircraft and rifle fire. Bullets seared through the metal skin of the C-47s, resulting in heavy damage to thirteen of them and causing one to crash. Twenty-five others also took hits from shrapnel and bullets. The canvas covering of the still-airborne gliders was little refuge for the glidermen, who held their rifles in front of them, unable to respond to their attackers. As bullets tore into bodies of some glidermen, others made heroic efforts to halt the flow of blood with tourniquets.

The concentration of enemy fire caused surviving members of the serial to become disorganized and begin dispersing. Nevertheless, they maintained enough order to effect a released attack in two organized columns from altitudes of 400 to 500 feet. Unable to follow the preferred procedure of first circling their targeted fields, the gliders attacked straight in, crashing into anything in their paths, including one another. The postage-stamp size fields were much too small to land in safely. Some gliders crashed directly into hedgerows studded with trees and at least half of the crashes were in fields heavily spiked with Rommel's Asparagus. Wings were ripped off and gliders were split open. One glider slammed into a herd of grazing cattle. Some crash landings were so severe that the lashings holding down the jeeps broke loose, obliterating the interior of the gliders and crushing men. The cry for a medic was heard time and again among the bloodied glidermen with their scattered equipment and destroyed gliders.

Notwithstanding the relentless antiaircraft fire, the poor visibility, the inadequate landing spaces, and the gauntlet of ground obstacles, between seventeen and twenty-three gliders actually landed on the targeted LZ. Almost all the gliders and eleven of the twenty-two jeeps were destroyed. The 57 mm antitank guns proved to be tough; all eight that landed within two miles of the LZ were fully operable, but two of them were stuck in gliders that had crashed in flooded areas around the Merderet River. The glidermen worked frantically to extricate their weapons and equipment and to assemble into a fighting unit.

Some paratroopers who saw the gliders land ran to their assistance and helped pry out

The Glider Assault on Normandy

the artillery pieces. Until then the airborne troops had not had any artillery in the area. By noon the artillery pieces were firing away at German positions, and they were still the only ones in action miles inland from the beaches of the American seaborne invasion.

The durability of the glidermen of the 82nd proved to be higher than that of their gliders and much of the equipment they brought with them. Among the casualties there were three glidermen killed and twenty-three severely injured. This total, however, does not take into account the numerous other wounds that were sustained by glidermen who continued on with their mission.

Glider landing sites in Normandy fields. (Silent Wings Museum)

Mission Keokuk was the next to go, beginning at 6:30 P.M., 6 June. Takeoff was from the same steel runway in Aldermaston that Mission Chicago had used just seventeen hours before. However, a key change in the plans for both Keokuk and Elmira was implemented to avoid continuing to expose the glidermen to the intense German antiaircraft fire that had beset the gliders of Chicago and Detroit. The flight path of those first two missions had approached the Cotentin Peninsula from the west coast. A revised flight plan for Keokuk and Elmira would have the gliders approach the peninsula from the east coast. This should reduce their vulnerability to German antiaircraft fire because they would pass over the American troops occupying Utah Beach.

Keokuk was to be the first daylight mission and the first glider attack using only the big wooden Horsas, or as they were also known, "English coffins." Thirty-two C-47s towed Horsas in what turned out to be an easy mission from the flight crew's perspective. The combination of good weather and daylight all the way to France contributed to keeping the formations organized and all participants on course. Squadrons of American fighters flew cover and no enemy fighters showed up to challenge. Release was scheduled for 9:00 P.M.; however, the serial arrived at the targeted LZ seven minutes early, at which time the gliders started to cut loose for their attack. The enemy had by then almost a full day of experience with the American glidermen. The Germans held two strongholds in close proximity to Keokuk's LZ, one located two miles to the south at St.-Côme-du-Mont and the other two miles to the north at Turqueville. This time, instead of firing on the tow planes, they held their fire while the tow planes passed over and then unloaded on the slowly descending gliders. Inaccurate glider landings may have helped to keep events from turning into a greater calamity. The Germans opened fire on the circling gliders, but most of the gliders were out of range of their guns.

The salvos of bullets fired at the ungainly Horsas punched through the wooden walls and ripped into glidermen. One bullet hit a gliderman in the knee, another blasted into a man's face. Other men whipped off their seatbelts and while trying to maintain their balance climbed over the equipment lashed to the floor to get to their wounded comrades. More bullets struck a gliderman in the back and another in the neck. Some of the gliders hit the ground and skidded into huge trees, mashing in their nose sections and fracturing the wooden fuselages into deadly splinters that impaled some glidermen. Survivors grabbed their weapons and tried to pull the wounded from the wreckage or tried to retrieve their howitzers and jeeps.

For the most part the clumsy Horsas of Mission Keokuk achieved good landings, with the exception of some critical accidents. Only five gliders landed on target and fourteen gliders ended up about two and a half miles northeast of their targeted LZ. Five more were scattered several hundred yards further east and eight were spread out up to two miles southeast of the LZ. Fourteen glidermen were killed by enemy fire and accidents. Thirty glidermen were seriously injured and ten more were missing and presumed to have been captured.

At 6:30 P.M., as Mission Keokuk was commencing at Aldermaston, the glidermen of the 82nd Airborne were preparing to undertake the biggest glider mission of them all. Mission Elmira involved 176 gliders that would take off from four different airfields according to exacting timetables. Elmira was divided into two echelons of seventy-six and one hundred gliders, respectively. Each echelon was further split into two serials. The first serial of echelon one was scheduled to take off at 6:40 P.M., 6 June, from Ramsbury, while the second serial was timed to take off ten minutes later from Greenham Commons in Berkshire. The two serials of the second echelon would take off two hours later from airfields at Membury and Welford, both also in Berkshire.

All glidermen were accounted for and equipment was on board when the lead tow plane and glider of the first serial of Mission Elmira charged down the runway at Ramsbury at 6:48 P.M. Twenty-six gliders comprised of eighteen Horsas and eight Wacos took to the sky. At 7:07 P.M. the lead tow plane and glider of the second serial raced down the Greenham Commons runway. Thirty-six Horsas and fourteen Wacos left the ground. All seventy-six gliders of Elmira's first echelon were airborne and on their way to attack Normandy by 7:21 P.M., D-Day.

The weather over the Channel was good, with excellent visibility. Squadrons of fighters showed up to provide escort. There was not much talking among the glidermen, who held their weapons in front of them and waited for the inevitable landing. The targeted LZ was six miles inland. Release altitudes varied from 500 to 750 feet. From that altitude a Waco could glide over two miles, but a loaded Horsa less than one. Unknown to the glidermen, their release point turned out to be directly over enemy strongpoints. Just as the gliders released to begin their attack, the Germans let go a bombardment of antiaircraft fire, using everything from rifles and machine guns to antitank guns against the gliders

Weapons and equipment of the glidermen of 2nd Battalion, 325th Glider Infantry Regiment, 82nd Airborne Division, await loading aboard a Horsa glider at Upottery Field, England, for the Normandy attack. (Silent Wings Museum)

Glidermen conduct a final check of their equipment moments before boarding their Horsa glider at Upottery Field for Normandy attack. Note the gliderman checking a bazooka at center left. (Silent Wings Museum)

and their departing C-47s. One tow plane alone was perforated with sixty-five bullet holes.

The gliders had neither darkness nor surprise on their side. Shrapnel lacerated the canvas skin of the Wacos. The top of one gliderman's head was blown off. Bullets ricocheted off equipment and tore into bodies. Glidermen jumped to the aid of their fellows, unbalancing the already wobbling aircraft. Equipment and helmets flew everywhere. Pilots aimed their gliders straight in for crash landings, but many of the designated landing fields, when they became visible, were only 600 feet long and flooded or were bordered by fifty-foot trees and spiked with Rommel's Asparagus.

Some Horsas cracked into trees, telescoping the cockpits and crushing the pilots. One Horsa crashed next to a burning tank, and seconds after the surviving glidermen escaped

Glider attack on D-Day. Some American glidermen in both Horsas and CG-4As having already landed, more gliders continue to cut loose to commence their attack. (National Archives)

it ignited. Many Horsas broke into pieces upon impact with trees or antiglider poles or fell apart from the force of the landing itself. One glider, attempting to negotiate the antiglider poles, had both wings stripped off and fishtailed down the field, banging around the glidermen inside. Another glider crashed next to a pillbox and another into the wing of an already collapsed glider.

To complicate matters, the fields had been sighted in by German guns prior to the assault. The glidermen were under fire even before their gliders had come to a halt and had to fight their way out of the wreckage of the gliders amid mortar and artillery bursts. Equipment, ammunition, broken crates, and bodies were scattered all around. Enemy sniper and machine-gun fire concentrated on the gliders, giving the glidermen a chance to seek cover in the nearest ditch until dark, when they could begin unloading the operable remnants of their cargo.

In the first serial, two gliders made it to the LZ, while a dozen more came within a mile. All but one or two of the others landed within two miles of it. In the second serial, twenty-two gliders landed on or very near the LZ, six came within a mile of it, and four more landed within three miles. The rest were scattered about. Eighty percent of the Horsas and almost half of the Wacos were damaged, many as a consequence of enemy fire. Three Wacos and twenty-one Horsas were destroyed. The glider pilot casualties were five killed, seventeen severely wounded, and four missing and presumed to have been captured. The glidermen of the 82nd fared little better. Five were killed and eighteen were severely wounded.

The glidermen who flew in the second echelon of Elmira would find enemy territory to be even less inviting than the first echelon had just hours before. The two Wacos and forty-eight Horsas of the first serial of Elmira's second echelon took off from the runway at

Horsa glider on its way to Normandy on D-Day. Tow ropes are clearly visible. (National Archives)

The Glider Assault on Normandy

71

Membury at 8:37 P.M., followed just three minutes later by the second serial, comprised of twelve Wacos and thirty-eight Horsas, from the airfield at Welford. The assault had been timed to take place in darkness and the sun was setting as the two serials passed over Utah Beach.

Only three miles inland the gliders were unexpectedly sprayed with the heaviest barrage of fire encountered by any serial that day. In the first serial alone, thirty-three of the fifty C-47s were hit, and in the second serial, three C-47s were forced to ditch in the Channel. The lead glider of the first serial released to start its attack at 10:55 P.M., a full five minutes ahead of schedule. The lead glider of the second serial released at 11:05 P.M. Again enemy fire riddled the gliders, only this time the glider pilots found even smaller fields, some only 300 feet long, in their LZ. Although under specific orders to land their big Horsas at slow speed, many of the pilots flew in at a 100 mph. Besides the relentless enemy fire, they found impenetrable walls of trees and deadly hedgerows at the end of each short field.

Demolished Horsa glider. The plywood frame has disintegrated. (Silent Wings Museum)

Glidermen were slaughtered in their seats, still holding on to their rifles. Shell fragments burst through the floor, through their boots, and into their feet. Gliders smashed into hedgerows, tossing men around like dolls. One glider crashed into the roof of a farmhouse, another spun out of control into a ditch. Some of the Horsas ruptured on impact, lancing glidermen with wooden splinters. After one Waco collided to a stop, snipers began firing into it. The glidermen inside responded by blindly firing back through the canvas walls, emptying their rifles and a BAR until only scraps of canvas were left hanging on the tubular frame. The sniper fire ceased. In the dark glidermen pulled their wounded out and ran to the nearest ditch for cover. Unloading the gliders was impossible but groups of glidermen assembled into combat teams.

In the first serial many of the gliders were released a mile or more short of the LZ, while six gliders were released five miles east of the target. The second serial was much more accurate, the majority of the gliders having landed within a mile of the LZ. Between

Reconnaissance photo of glider landings taken just hours after opening attack on D-Day. Note the many smashed gliders, both Horsas and CG-4As, some of which crashed into one another and others that disintegrated upon impact into hedgerows. (U.S. Air Force Photo Collection [USAF Neg. No. 51750 AC], courtesy of National Air and Space Museum, Smithsonian Institution)

the extremely heavy enemy fire and the toll taken by crashes, fifty-six of the eighty-six Horsas in the second echelon were wrecked and only thirteen were left in one piece. Not one of the fourteen Wacos survived the ordeal intact and eight of them were destroyed. Equipment fared better than the gliders in Mission Elmira. Forty-two jeeps, twenty-eight trailers, and fifteen of the twenty-four howitzers were operable and ready for action. Casualties were heavy. Ten glider pilots were killed, twenty-nine were seriously wounded, and another seven were captured and taken prisoner. Twenty-eight glidermen were killed and another 107 were seriously wounded. The rest of the glidermen, many bloodied and some wearing makeshift tourniquets, formed up into fighting units and continued the fight.

Although Mission Elmira concluded the American glider missions of D-Day, the glider attacks were far from over and would continue the next day as scheduled. From London an official announcement of the invasion was flashed over radio waves to the world: "This is Supreme Headquarters Allied Expeditionary Force. Under the command of General Eisenhower, Allied naval forces supported by strong air forces began landing Allied armies this morning on the northern coast of France." Also on D-Day, President Roosevelt delivered the following prayer to the world:

> Almighty God: Our sons, pride of our nation this day have set upon a mighty endeavor, a struggle to preserve our republic, our religion and our civilization, and to set free a suffering humanity.
> Give strength to their arms, stoutness to their hearts, steadfastness to their faith.
> Their road will be long and hard. For the enemy is strong. He may hurl back our forces. Success may not come with rushing speed, but we shall return again and again and we know that by the grace and the righteousness of our cause, our sons will triumph.
> They will be sore tried by night and by day, without rest until the victory is won. The darkness will be rent by noise and flame. Men's souls will be shaken with the violences of war. For these men are drawn from the ways of peace. They fight not for the lust of conquest, they fight to end conquest. They fight to liberate. They fight to let justice arise among all Thy people. They yearn but for the end of battle, for their return to the haven of home. Some will never return. Embrace these, Father, and receive them, Thy heroic servants into Thy kingdom. . . .[1]

In the early hours of D plus one, Missions Galveston and Hackensack were to deliver all the firepower of the 82nd Airborne's 325th Glider Infantry Regiment. At 2:00 A.M., 7 June, whistles were blown simultaneously at Ramsbury and Aldermaston. The men had tried to get some rest before their inevitable call to arms. They were fully dressed and all the weapons and gear they had been issued were beside them. Rising to their feet in the cool, early morning air, they moved in orderly fashion through latrine and chow lines. The general feeling was much the same as before other glider takeoffs, except perhaps that everyone seemed a little quieter. Every conceivable detail had already been attended to, so there was little cause for confusion. There were also numerous photographers around to take pictures of the start of the historic mission. The battle that the glidermen were about to engage in would be the toughest and most important that their regiment had ever fought.

No one lingered over breakfast and the ham and eggs were consumed quickly. A few whispers, the shuffling of feet, and the dull clanking of utensils against the mess kits were about the only sounds. At 2:30 A.M. the men secured their equipment. Each company formed into platoons, squads and equipment were checked, the men accounted for, the weapons and gear made ready. At 3:00 A.M. the order was given and the men marched in

1. *Chicago Daily Tribune*, 6 June 1944, p. 2.

silent formation out to the runway where their gliders were waiting. Each man's load must have felt a little heavier, with the extra bandolier of ammo, an extra grenade, a pistol, and everything else that had been stuffed in his pack. By 3:30 A.M. a light drizzle had started to fall as the glidermen lined up in front of their gliders.

Mission Galveston was to begin with two serials of fifty gliders each taking off concurrently from two different airfields. The first serial, leaving from Ramsbury, was comprised of thirty-two Wacos and eighteen Horsas. All fifty gliders in the second serial, leaving from Aldermaston, were Wacos. The time for takeoff had been scheduled for 4:30 A.M., more than half an hour before dawn. By then the weather had taken a turn for the worse, with rain, gusty winds, and very poor visibility. At 4:32 A.M. the first glider of the mission became airborne from the Aldermaston airfield, slicing through rain and a strong wind. At 4:39 A.M. the wheels of the lead glider at airfield Ramsbury left the ground, fighting the same treacherous weather.

Many of the gliders were crammed with excessive loads. Fighting the wind and the extra weight, one tow plane could not pull an overloaded Horsa fast enough to achieve takeoff speed and had to cut the glider loose. The glidermen aboard were fortunate that their pilot was able to stop the big glider at the end of the runway. After becoming airborne, another glider was accidentally released while attempting to join in formation. Two more Horsas struggled to stay airborne and the tow planes were unable to achieve the designated altitudes of their formations. The rain and wind buffeted the gliders and tossed the men around.

Aboard one glider a box of antitank rifle grenades broke loose and slammed into two men. In another glider the retaining block on the front of a howitzer came loose and the gun rolled forward, the barrel smashing into the glider's frame and punching a hole in the

Crashed Horsa glider that has broken in two. (Silent Wings Museum)

cloth wall. The wind blowing furiously expanded the gaping hole, adding still more drag to the already chugging tow plane. The glidermen tried to brace the front wheels of the artillery piece by moving boxes of mines and artillery shells around it.

Another Horsa could not maintain altitude and began pulling against its tow plane. Someone aboard the glider yelled at the men to lighten the load. As the plane continued to descend rapidly, to less than 300 feet, they forced open the door and began dumping boxes of mines, crates of grenades, mortar shells, and cans of water. The glider hit an air pocket that knocked them off their feet and one man almost fell through the door before two others grabbed him. Slowly but perceptibly the lightened glider started to gain altitude and join the rear of the glider train.

As the formations approached the Channel, the rain stopped, the weather improved, and the clouds broke, giving way to excellent visibility and revealing an enormous number of ships below. Looking out a small porthole at the Allied naval armada, one gliderman commented that it looked like you couldn't "drop a rock without hitting a boat." Seeing the size of the fleet gave many of the men a greater sense of confidence.

As the serials flew over the French coastline they were immediately hit with rifle and machine-gun fire. The first glider of each serial released to commence their attacks at 6:55 A.M. and 7:01 A.M., respectively. In an attempt to avoid the continuing ground fire, many of the tow planes of the first serial brought their gliders in at extremely low altitudes, releasing them at only 100 to 300 feet above the ground. From those altitudes the range of the gliders was not much more than half a mile, or about thirty seconds in the air. The gliders attacked straight in, landing one right after another. As one glider would crash, the next would have no time to avert the wreckage and would smash into it. Others crashed into antiglider poles that ripped off wings and sent fuselages spinning wildly. One glider landing in a small open field slid on the ground some distance before hitting a mine and exploding.

A Horsa failed to clear a hedgerow between adjacent fields and its belly was torn open, crushing the glidermen and equipment inside. Another Horsa lost one of its wings when it collided with an antiglider asparagus, then veered directly into a stone wall and virtually disintegrated. One glider pilot avoided hitting the wreck in front of him by crashing into an embankment. The right wing fractured and the glider rolled over on its side, spilling a jeep onto a gliderman and crushing him. Sniper fire from a hedgerow began hitting the jeep. While three glidermen returned fire, two others worked to pry the man out.

In the first serial of Galveston, seventeen of the eighteen Horsas were damaged, ten of them being destroyed. Nine Wacos were wrecked and another fifteen were damaged. Due to the low release altitudes, the majority of the gliders missed their LZ. Most of the gliders in the second serial were released at higher altitudes and therefore had more accurate landings. Twenty of them landed on the LZ, nineteen within approximately a mile of it, and eight within two miles. Sixteen Wacos were destroyed and another twenty-six were damaged. Notwithstanding the magnitude of the destruction, Galveston had delivered a number of operable jeeps and trailers, as well as seven artillery pieces. However, seventeen glidermen were killed and another eighty-five were severely wounded.

The stage was set for the final glider assault of Operation Neptune into Nazi territory. Mission Hackensack would utilize over 1,300 glidermen, the bulk of the 325th Glider Infantry Regiment. Hackensack was timed to begin two hours later than Galveston. Two se-

Burning remains of a crashed glider on D-Day. (Silent Wings Museum)

rials consisting of fifty gliders each would take off simultaneously from Upottery in Devonshire and Merryfield in Somerset. At 2:30 A.M. the whistles blew at both bases, signaling the moment they had been waiting for.

Serial one, leaving from Upottery, consisted of thirty Horsas and twenty Wacos carrying a total of 968 glidermen from the 2nd Battalions of both the 325th and the 401st—the latter having been attached to the 325th as its third battalion. More than 800 of the glidermen would fly in Horsas. That serial was to concentrate on delivering assault troops, and matériel was limited to just five vehicles, eleven tons of ammunition, and ten tons of miscellaneous supplies. The second serial, from Merryfield, consisted of fifty Wacos that would carry 363 glidermen, primarily from the service units of the 325th and the 401st. That serial would carry more matériel, including twelve 81 mm mortars, twenty jeeps, nine trailers, six tons of ammunition, and eighteen additional tons of equipment, such as mines and antitank grenades.

A light rain was falling in the predawn hours when the command was given to move out to the runway. The men slogged across wet grass and patches of mud to the gliders. Climbing aboard with their heavy loads, some of them needed a push from behind. One man with some kind of a marker stopped long enough to write his name on the side of his glider, and the men around him followed suit. As each C-47 moved into position for take-off, 300 feet of tow rope bound it to its glider. At precisely 6:47 A.M. the first glider of Mission Hackensack left the runway at Upottery. Thirty minutes later, 7:17 A.M., the lead glider of the second serial took off from Merryfield.

Talk was restrained aboard the gliders as they pitched and rolled. Holding their rifles, some men stared off into space, as if in deep meditation. Others may have been praying. At least one man was reading from a New Testament that a chaplain had given him back at Fort Bragg. Another gliderman yelled out, "Is this trip really necessary?" which brought chuckles from the others around him.

The clouds thinned out over the Channel, and as the glider train approached Normandy, visibility became excellent. A large fighter escort accompanied the formations. The first glider of serial one released to begin its attack at 8:51 A.M., nine minutes ahead of schedule. The second serial began its attack at 8:59 A.M., eleven minutes early. Releases were effected from an altitude of 600 feet. No enemy fire had been encountered so far. The gliders veered off from their formations and circled the small fields to seek safe places to land. As they slowly descended to about 300 feet, the German gunners below unleashed a blistering barrage of gunfire. The Germans fired directly up into the exposed undersides of gliders that were passing just a few feet overhead. Bullets pierced the floors of the aircraft and burrowed into the bodies of glidermen. Men, spattered with blood, tried to render assistance to wounded comrades. Glider pilots frantically maneuvered to land without crashing into one another.

One Horsa took a broadside of fire just as it was about to crash-land. Bullets crackled through the wooden walls and blasted into several men. Although off balance, two glidermen managed to push open the door of the still speeding glider so that another could fire his BAR out the opening. One of the wings clipped an antiglider pole and was partly torn off, causing the glider to veer into the tail of a downed Waco, then into a hedgerow. As another Horsa attempted to miss an antiglider pole, it smashed into the wall of a house. Yet another Horsa, riddled with bullet holes, attempted a landing in a tiny field and skidded directly into a large tree, killing the pilot instantly in the mangled forward section. The rest of the craft buckled up and broke in half as it continued to plow through the trees, finally breaking up into splinters.

One Waco stayed aloft long enough to avoid crashing into a Horsa, only to have its wings sliced off by an antiglider pole and set off the explosion of a mine. Another glider took so many hits in its wings and tail that the pilot lost all control, causing the glider to pitch forward and nose-dive into the ground. Men and equipment were scattered all about

American glidermen ready for battle dash from the open door of their Horsa glider immediately upon landing in Normandy. (Silent Wings Museum)

and a dead cow lay where it had been killed by a Horsa. Glidermen clawed their way out of their demolished craft under scorching machine-gun fire and mortar blasts to rescue the wounded or to go after the snipers and the machine-gun nests embedded in the hedgerows. The survivors fought back tenaciously, some even jumping out of gliders that were still skidding across fields. Several other gliders crashed into marshlands that had been flooded by the enemy and sank into waist-deep water, drowning glidermen whose wounds and heavy equipment prevented their escape.

Of the gliders accounted for, the first serial landed nineteen within a mile of their targeted LZ, thirteen within two miles, fifteen from two to four miles away, and one nine miles away. The second serial, consisting entirely of Wacos, was extremely accurate. At least twenty-five gliders hit the targeted LZ, nineteen landed within a mile, and the other half dozen were not much farther off. Although the scene on the ground gave the appearance of a massacre, Hackensack turned out to be a remarkable success. Most of the glidermen were delivered to the battlefield, together with eighteen jeeps and eight trailers in operable, combat-ready condition, as well as much of the other cargo of ammunition, mortars, and supplies. Ten Horsas were damaged and sixteen others were demolished. Ten Wacos were damaged, while four were destroyed. Hackensack casualties included two pilots killed and eleven others severely injured, plus fifteen glidermen killed and fifty-nine others severely wounded. Many of the rest sustained multiple injuries but were considered able to continue their engagement with the enemy.

9

Dead American glidermen laid in front of their crashed Horsa glider on D-Day. (National Archives)

After-Action Considerations

DESPITE ALL THE CRASH LANDINGS and the innumerable firefights with enemy troops in the fields, the glidermen of the 325th Glider Infantry Regiment had completely assembled themselves into an effective combat force by 10:15 A.M., 7 June. Almost ninety percent of the regiment was still capable of fighting. The 1st Battalion reported 545 men ready for action, the 2nd Battalion 624 men, and the 3rd Battalion 550 men. The glidermen were immediately sent into battle in a campaign that lasted for thirty-three days.

Leigh-Mallory's dire predictions had proved inaccurate. No one will ever know, of course, whether the lower number of casualties was the result of luck, fate, training, or some combination thereof. It should be remembered, however, that Bradley never disputed Leigh-Mallory's casualty estimates; indeed he was willing to accept seventy percent casualties among the glidermen, if that were what it took to secure Utah Beach. In fact the glider mission landing casualties ran about eleven percent, which is somewhat deceptive because it is the statistical average of all six glider missions. Some companies sustained casualties of approximately twenty-five percent during landing—a high price to pay in order to get soldiers to the battlefield. Among the gliders, ninety-seven percent were no longer combat-worthy and were left to rot where they landed. By the end of D-Day alone, the 82nd Airborne counted 1,259 of its men either killed, wounded, or missing in action, and the casualties sustained by the 101st were almost identical at 1,240.

The question that begs to be answered is whether or not the risks taken by the glidermen and paratroopers and the losses that resulted were worth the gain. A comparison of the Utah and Omaha landings seems to vindicate Bradley's intractable demand for airborne support at Utah, suggesting that the role of the airborne forces was critical in determining the success achieved in the American sector of the invasion. When the American invasion force landed on Utah Beach on 6 June at 6:30 A.M., there was no significant opposition to confront them, other than a few long-range artillery shells. By the end of D-Day 22,000 GIs and 1,800 vehicles were securely ashore on Utah. The men had moved inland rapidly, seizing ground and working to link up with their airborne comrades, who had blocked the enemy from the beaches and were still locked in combat with them. Among the entire Utah seaborne invasion force there were 197 casualties, sixty of whom were killed in the Channel when their boats were sunk. The casualties, in other words, were light for an invasion of that size.

The events of D-Day at Omaha Beach, where no glidermen or paratroopers were sent in behind enemy lines, were disastrous. American soldiers were killed in the water or were pinned down on the beach and against the cliffs by enemy crossfire. Calls had to be made for artillery support from the ships offshore. Men clawed their way forward, trying to get a foothold, and finally fought their way off the beach and onto the bluffs above. By the end of the day the seaborne assault troops had only advanced a mile and a half inland. The D-Day casualty list for "Bloody Omaha" totaled 2,374 men killed, wounded, or missing in action.

Glidermen inspect a Horsa glider that snapped in half upon landing during D-Day attack. (Silent Wings Museum)

Glidermen examine a collapsed Horsa glider on D-Day. (National Archives)

Horses and cows return to a French pasture used by a Horsa glider as a landing field on D-Day. (U.S. Air Force Photo Collection [USAF Neg. No. 53206 AC], courtesy of National Air and Space Museum, Smithsonian Institution)

Clearly there were many other differences between the landings at Omaha and Utah, including the terrain and the enemy's position and strength. Whether the use of airborne troops could have helped to reduce the number of casualties on Omaha can never be known for certain. However, it is worth noting the "Representation of the Events" reported to German headquarters on 10 June by the chief of staff of the German 7th Army, which opposed the Allied invasion forces: "The superior navy and air force have given the enemy advantages which cannot be compensated for, even through strong fortifications. The operation of the 'new weapon,' the airborne troops, behind the coastal fortifications, on one hand, and their massive attack on our own counterattacking troops, on the other hand, have contributed significantly to the initial success of the enemy."[1]

In his 25 July report to the Allied supreme commander, the division commander of the 82nd Airborne had this to say about the invasion:

> Landing during darkness, beginning at H-4 hours on D-Day, this division partici-
> pated in the initial operations of the invasion of Western Europe for thirty-three
> continuous days without relief and without replacements. It accomplished every
> assigned mission on or ahead of the time ordered. No ground gained was ever relin-
> quished and no advance ever halted except on the order of Corps or Army. It sus-
> tained an aggregate loss of 46 per cent in killed, missing, and evacuated wounded.
> Prior to launching its final offensive, its infantry had sustained a loss of 45 per cent.
> At the conclusion of its operation it went into Army reserve, with fighting spirit
> as high as the day it entered action.[2]

1. Gavin, *On to Berlin,* p. 121.
2. Gavin, *On to Berlin,* p. 120.

After-Action Considerations

Cows in a field where a CG-4A glider landed on D-Day. (National Archives)

Plans were already in the works for the next glider assault, which involved seizing a series of bridges over rivers and canals in Holland, thereby enabling the main body of the Allied forces to continue their advance into Germany. Code-named "Operation Market Garden," the assault would begin 17 September 1944.

By definition, being a soldier in combat is always a dangerous occupation. However, the army decided to pay additional compensation to those soldiers who were deemed to be involved in particularly hazardous undertakings. GI remuneration was notoriously paltry and hazardous duty pay added up to a little more money. But there was more at issue than simply more money for cigarettes and poker. On a more fundamental level, it meant some acknowledgement of the degree of danger that the men who received it were actually involved in and some tribute to their skill and bravery in combat. As important as the extra pay was, to many men an equal if not more compelling reason to be classified as entitled to receive hazardous duty pay was that intangible element of recognition from both one's peers and superiors for the risks one was taking.

At the time of the invasion of Normandy, the paratroopers of Operation Neptune were ordered to receive hazardous duty pay, as were the flight crews of the C-47s that towed the glidermen into combat. Their activities were deemed to merit the additional stipend. Glidermen, however, were not legally entitled to receive hazardous duty pay. The act of entering combat behind enemy lines, inside of a canvas covered, unarmed, unarmored, engineless aircraft had not been considered to be dangerous enough to warrant hazardous duty pay. Neither were they given parachutes, which the flight crews did receive.

Glider snap takeoff. One of the few CG-4A gliders in retrievable condition stands ready for the first snap takeoff since its D-Day landing. The line between the two upright poles is about to be caught by a hook underneath the C-47, at which time the poles will collapse. (National Archives)

Such a myopic conclusion could only have been based upon the fallacy that flying in a combat glider was just another way to go to war. The military had formed this conclusion using criteria that applied to the usual risk faced by troops whenever they were transported from any point A to any point B. However, it is inconceivable how anyone could believe that attacking such a highly trained, sophisticated, and mechanized enemy by means of an unpowered *glider* would carry no greater risk than being transported by train or some form of armored personnel carrier. Flying into combat in a "tow target" or "flying coffin" was just not the same as going by truck. Then again, no American general had ever gone into combat in a glider before Operation Neptune. The general who did so at Normandy was killed in a crash that earned him the distinction of becoming the first of his rank on either side to die on D-Day.

Paratroopers were also awarded the privilege of wearing a special badge, their coveted Paratrooper Badge that was cast in sterling silver and had the emblem of a parachute in the center of wings. The glidermen had not been granted a similar recognition. Not only was this perceived to be a brazen injustice by the highly trained glidermen, but many of their fellow paratroopers and troop carrier brethren agreed.

One month after D-Day, in July 1944, the dishonorable situation was finally rectified. The glidermen were ordered to receive the same hazardous duty pay as the paratroopers,

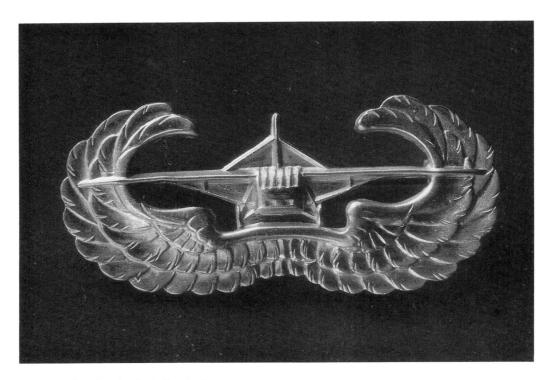

Glider Badge. (Author's Collection)

$50 per month for an enlisted man and $100 per month for an officer. Even more important to many glidermen, they were awarded their own badge. The sterling silver Glider Badge was about one and a half inches wide and about five-eighths of an inch high. It was almost identical in appearance to the paratrooper's badge, which was done deliberately to accord the fullest possible recognition to the glidermen and to firmly establish absolute parity between the two airborne branches. The only difference between the badges was that the parachute had been eliminated from the gliderman's badge and in its place was engraved the front view of a Waco glider.

"Glidermen" does not even appear in the dictionary. Yet these were men who fought for their country by soaring into the most technologically sophisticated warfare the world had ever known, aboard fragile, unarmed, cloth-covered and wooden aircraft. Their very existence in that highly mechanized and armored global conflict was enigmatic. But the fact of their existence stands as a tribute to their courage.

Edith Steiger Phillips was a Red Cross volunteer who witnessed the return from the front of men from the 325th Glider Infantry Regiment. In her book *My World War II Diary* she writes:

We stood so alone under the only light at the Leicester railway station the night the 325 men returned after thirty-three days of battle without relief. It was Sunday, 9th July, and the night was pitch black. The light we stood under must have been a twenty-five watt. It gave so little light I could not recognize any of the men as they marched by us. When I asked Colonel Lewis how many men were returning, he got all choked up. He wasn't too sure but he thought about a third! I was prepared for a few hundred but a third, never!

The soldiers got off the train slowly and walked up the stairs like tired old men. I strained my eyes to recognize a face but didn't see anybody I knew. The men were unshaven, mud-caked and they slumped.

Back at the camp that night Colonel Lewis insisted on going to the mess hall where the men were to be fed but a coughing spell racked him and he had to sit down on the ground. He leaned on the driver and me and went to his HQ shack where he put his head on his arms to get comfortable at his small desk. I left the Colonel and ran to the mess hall to help pour coffee but the men just sat there staring into space. They didn't eat. They fell asleep at the table. I didn't say a word to anybody. I noticed, however, that the GIs sat here, there and everywhere in the hall as though returning to a place where they had sat before. I dare not ask where this or that boy was. I knew."[3]

3. Deryk Wills, *Put on Your Boots and Parachutes!* (Leicester, Eng.: Deryk Wills, 1992), p. 115, quoting Edith S. Phillips, *My World War II Diary* (n.p., n.d.).

Bibliography
Index

Bibliography

"The All-American: 82nd Airborne Division Anniversary Edition," *Fort Bragg Post*, 25 March 1943.

"Beachheads of Normandy." *Life*, 19 June 1944, p. 25.

Blair, Clay. *Ridgway's Paratroopers*. New York: Doubleday, 1985.

Bradley, Omar N. *A Soldier's Story*. New York: Henry Holt, 1951.

Breuer, William B., *Hitler's Fortress Cherbourg*. New York: Stein and Day, 1984.

Churchill, Winston S. *Closing the Ring*. Boston: Houghton Mifflin, 1951. Vol. 5 of *The Second World War*.

————. *The Hinge of Fate*. Boston: Houghton Mifflin, 1950. Vol. 4 of *The Second World War*.

————. *Triumph and Tragedy*. Boston: Houghton Mifflin, 1953. Vol. 6 of *The Second World War*.

Crookenden, Napier. *Dropzone Normandy*. New York: Charles Scribner's Sons, 1976.

Dank, Milton. *The Glider Gang*. Philadelphia: J. B. Lippincott, 1977.

Dawson, W. Forrest. *Saga of the All Americans* (82nd Airborne Division). Privately published. Reprint, Nashville: Battery Press, 1946.

D'Este, Carlo. *Decision in Normandy*. New York: E. P. Dutton, 1983.

Devlin, Gerard M. *Silent Wings*. New York: St. Martin's Press, 1985.

Eisenhower, Dwight D. *Crusade in Europe*. New York: Doubleday, 1948.

Ellison, Norman. *British Gliders and Sailplanes, 1922–1970*. New York: Barnes and Noble, 1971.

Farrar-Hockley, Anthony. *Airborne Carpet: Operation Market Garden*. New York: Ballantine, 1969.

"Fierce Battle Rages in Normandie, Berlin Says." *Chicago Daily Tribune*, 6 June 1944, p. 1.

Gavin, James M. *On To Berlin*. New York: Bantam, 1985.

Gilbert, Martin. *The Second World War*. New York: Henry Holt, 1989.

Glider Diary 1, no. 1, 7 Jan. 1945. (Limited edition newspaper in author's collection.)

Hastings, Max. *Overlord D-Day and the Battle for Normandy*. New York: Simon and Schuster, 1984.

Hoyt, Edwin P. *The Invasion Before Normandy*. New York: Stein and Day, 1985.

Macdonald, John. *Great Battles of World War II*. Philadelphia: Running Press, 1993.

Manchester, William. *The Glory and the Dream: A Narrative History of America, 1932–1972*. Vol 1. Boston: Little, Brown, 1973.

Marshall, S. L. A. *Night Drop*. Nashville: Battery Press, 1962.

Martin, Ralph G., and Richard Harrity. *World War II: A Photographic Record of the War in Europe*. New York: Fawcett, 1962.

Mitcham, Samuel W., Jr. *Rommel's Last Battle*. New York: Stein and Day, 1983.

Mrazek, James E. *The Glider War*. New York: St. Martin's Press, 1975.

Norton, G. G. *The Red Devils*. London: Leo Cooper, 1971.

Pierce, Wayne. "Normandy! Let's Go!" *Silent Wings Museum Foundation, Museum News*, July–Aug. 1993, pp. 4–5.

Ryan, Cornelius. *The Longest Day*. New York: Simon and Schuster, 1959.

Shinkle, Florence. "The Day of the Big Glider Crash." *St. Louis Post-Dispatch*, 4 May 1975, pp. 4–14.

Thompson, Leroy. *The All Americans: The 82nd Airborne*. New York: Sterling, 1988.

Thompson, R. W. *D-Day: Spearhead of Invasion*. New York: Ballantine, 1968.

Weeks, John. *The Airborne Soldier*. Poole (Dorset), Eng.: Blandford, 1986.

———. *Assault from the Sky: The History of Airborne Warfare*. Trowbridge (Wiltshire), Eng.: David Charles, 1978.

Wertenbaker, Charles C. "The Big Days." *Life*, 19 June 1944, p. 32.

Wheal, Elizabeth-Ann, Stephen Pope, and James Taylor. *The Meridian Encyclopedia of the Second World War*. New York: Penguin, 1992.

Wills, Deryk. *Put on Your Boots and Parachutes!* Leicester, Eng.: Deryk Wills, 1992.

"Wing Falls Off at 2,000 Feet." *St. Louis Globe-Democrat*, 2 Aug. 1943, p. 1.

Wynn, Humphrey, and Susan Young. *Prelude to Overlord*. Novato, CA: Presidio, 1983.

Young, Peter, ed. *The World Almanac of World War II*. New York: Pharos, 1986.

Bibliography

Index

Index

Charles J. Masters is an attorney, author, and historian. A member of the Silent Wings Museum Foundation, he lives in Chicago.